Identity Excellence

Identity Excellence

A Theory of Moral Expertise for Higher Education

Perry L. Glanzer

ROWMAN & LITTLEFIELD
Lanham • Boulder • New York • London

Published by Rowman & Littlefield
An imprint of The Rowman & Littlefield Publishing Group, Inc.
4501 Forbes Boulevard, Suite 200, Lanham, Maryland 20706
www.rowman.com

86-90 Paul Street, London EC2A 4NE

British Library Cataloguing in Publication Information Available

Library of Congress Cataloging-in-Publication Data
Names: Glanzer, Perry L. (Perry Lynn), author.
Title: Identity excellence : a theory of moral expertise for higher education / Perry
    L. Glanzer.
Description: Lanham, Maryland : Rowman & Littlefield, 2022. | Includes bibliographical
    references and index.
Identifiers: LCCN 2022011993 (print) | LCCN 2022011994 (ebook) |
    ISBN 9781475865479 (cloth) | ISBN 9781475865486 (paperback) |
    ISBN 9781475865493 (ebook)
Subjects: LCSH: Education, Higher—Moral and ethical aspects—United States.
    | Education, Higher—Aims and objectives—United States. | Moral education
    (Higher)—United States. | Identity (Psychology)
Classification: LCC LB2324 .G533 2022 (print) | LCC LB2324 (ebook) |
    DDC 378.73—dc23/eng/20220427
LC record available at https://lccn.loc.gov/2022011993
LC ebook record available at https://lccn.loc.gov/2022011994

To David Lyle Jeffrey, thanks for your encouragement and example of what it means to be an excellent professor

Contents

Preface

The Results of Meta-Democratic Moral Education

with Katie Klingstedt

In recent interviews with first year undergraduates, I have noticed an emerging category of students with unique moral characteristics. Shaped by a peculiar form of K–12 moral education, they share a strong, principled concern for social justice, but it is often their only major moral concern. For instance, when asked about how to address disagreements with teachers or peers, one incoming student, Samantha, tells our interviewer, "I pretty much mind my own business, unless it's an issue like racism or sexism, because for those things, you have to be actively antiracist, not just not personally antiracist."

Yet, beyond a passion for a virtue associated with being an excellent citizen, these students have little to guide their other identities. For instance, when it comes to being an excellent student, they largely see cheating as unproblematic if it helps them reach their academic goals. Describing his experience with cheaters in high school, John relates, "I never joined them . . . unless it was last minute, and I was going to fail if I didn't have the assignment done." Similarly, Andre offers, "It's always gonna be in the back of my head that it's a bad idea," but there are many times where "it also seemed effective and efficient."

June has a process of moral reasoning that she engages in when deciding whether or not to cheat: "I think, will I really need this subject the rest of my life? For science classes, things like that, I would really study the material and try to really learn and not cheat because it had relevance to my life." All the students interviewed are quick to say that they feel cheating is bad. However, this feeling is easily overridden when cheating provides them a personal advantage. When it comes to being excellent students, these undergraduates lacked moral conviction.

This lack of moral conviction outside of one's political identity as a citizen and the virtue of social justice leaves them lacking moral consistency or moral answers in other parts of their life. For instance, when our interviewer asks Samantha about her purpose, her answers change throughout the interview. At first, she says, "What gives me value is my academic stuff . . . the entirety of my academic career, doing well on your tests makes you a more valuable student, and that kind of tied into me personally." Later, she mentioned that medicine is her purpose.

However, when we ask her about the good life, she does not mention medicine or grades, but instead speaks of family, work-life balance, safety, and happiness. Later, she even discusses Maslow's hierarchy of needs as the concept that guides her moral decision-making. She lacks a narrative to effectively tie her ideas together, and it leaves her uncertain of her purpose, her moral convictions, and how to talk about them.

Similarly, when asked about his reason for certain moral views, John shares, "I don't know how I came to that conclusion. I really don't. I have no idea." Andre, when questioned what gives his life purpose, he laughs and says, "You're asking me what is the meaning to life? I can't answer that! I haven't lived long enough to figure it out." June, who claims Christianity as her faith, simply identifies it as a "fallback," that gives her comfort, instead of an overarching metanarrative that guides her moral thoughts, affections, and actions.

As a result of these characteristics, these students lack the moral framework and concepts by which to analyze their moral lives beyond their political identities. They are unable to identify moral conflicts or challenges faced. When asked about moral habits they have developed, they are not even able to list one. When asked about the moral wisdom they have acquired, they point back to themselves. As one student confidently claimed, "I have a moral compass in my head, and it's usually pointed in the right direction."

Interestingly, all these students express, in different ways, that they make decisions based on the moral deservedness of the respondent. Thus, the students share things like "not everyone is worth my time and energy" and "kindness is not inherently good, not everyone is deserving of my kindness and time."

Furthermore, only a few of these students mention external moral influences or external moral mentors. Older adults for this group also appear undeserving of moral praise. The most revealing answer perhaps is in response to the question, "To whom or what are you accountable?" These students respond with "myself."

Overall, these new students appear to be guided by what, in a previous book, I identified as the story of Meta-Democracy, which prizes autonomy as one of its two major virtues (the other being social justice).[1] Consequently, these students look to themselves for moral answers and insight rather than others. They have successfully self-authored their moral lives.

As I continually evaluate these results, I think we must recognize the shortcomings with the self-authored lives our theories guiding moral education have produced. These approaches exalt the metademocratic identity and story and the associated virtues of autonomy and social justice, but they leave students without moral experts or guides to help them develop moral expertise in other areas of life. They also absolve us of moral accountability for their lives.

We need a theory that makes us, as educators, accountable as contributors to students' moral education and to the development of moral excellence in more than simply their political or professional identities. To deny this need is to forsake students' moral excellence and our own. This book attempts to provide that theory.

NOTE

1. Perry L. Glanzer, *The Dismantling of Moral Education: How Higher Education Reduced the Human Identity* (Lanham, MD: Rowman & Littlefield, 2022).

Acknowledgments

I would like to thank all the identity mentors I have had throughout my life who have taught me identity excellence in my various identities: my parents who taught me excellence as an image bearer of God and parenting; the members of the First Baptist Church of Belton who taught me to be a better member of Christ's body; my brother who taught me to use my nondominant left hand to be a better basketball player, and still teaches me about being an excellent brother; Mark Mahler who models excellent friendship; Thomas Haskell who taught me to be an excellent student; my wife who exemplifies what it means to be an excellent neighbor; my whole extended family who taught me in various ways how to be an excellent family member and husband; Rick Hove who introduced me to what it means to be an excellent steward of finances; Wai Lim who taught me to be a better member of Christ's universal body; Stanley Hauerwas who illuminated a better way to thinking about being an excellent citizen.

In addition, I am grateful to Jessica Martin for offering numerous broad insights and editorial suggestions that influenced the shape of the final manuscript.

PERMISSIONS

Original portions of this book were previously published in academic journals. A portion of chapter 1 originally appeared in Perry L. Glanzer, "Building the Good Life: Using Identities to Frame Moral Education in Higher Education," *Journal of College and Character* 14:2 (May 2013): 177–84. An original version of chapter 4 appeared in Perry L. Glanzer, "General Education Sucks: So Teach the Great Identities," *Journal of General Education* 69, no. 3 4 (2020): pp. 179–195. I am grateful to the publishers for permission to reprint these pages.

Introduction

Higher Education's Confusion about Moral Expertise

Most social situations are not moral, because there is no conflict between the role-taking expectations of one person and another.

—Lawrence Kohlberg[1]

Moral dilemmas have a way of capturing our imaginations. "What would I do in that situation?" we ask ourselves. The popularity of seemingly impossible decisions constructed by moral philosophers or psychologists bear this out. For example, in 2016, the famous trolley problem originally set forth by Philippa Foot in 1967, received attention on the television show *The Good Place*.[2] In the trolley problem, a person must choose how to steer a runaway trolley. The person can choose to let the trolley run its course and kill four people or one can consciously steer it so that it kills only one person.

In the show, a demon named Michael helps a Nigerian-born moral philosophy professor named Chidi recreate the trolley problem as a real experience. The characters are forced to experience the trolley problem repeatedly, like in the movie *Groundhog Day*, and are forced to make a decision (which Chidi, the moral philosophy professor, has a hard time doing). As they keep going through the scenario, Michael asks Chidi, "Why don't you just tell me the right answer?" Chidi responds, "That's what's so great about the trolley problem, that there is no right answer." To which Michael responds, "This is why everyone hates moral philosophy professors."[3]

Indeed, ethicists deserve reproach if they primarily spend time asking students to discuss difficult moral dilemmas. Approaches to moral philosophy and moral psychology focused on dilemmas are the result of a view, similar

1

to Kohlberg's, depicted in the epigraph above. In this view, moral and ethical issues primarily relate to moral conflicts and not moral excellence.

Yet, anyone pursuing the good life should realize that Kohlberg is wrong. Although conflicts between our identities and various ethical components of what it means to be excellent in those identities play a key role, the moral life is not simply about moral conflict. Moral dilemmas are occasional, whereas the pursuit of excellence should be an all-consuming part of life. Thus, any approach to the good life needs to start by talking about moral excellence and the expertise one needs to achieve excellence.

Students and parents may think that higher education would be an important place where future leaders would acquire moral expertise. After all, professors usually teach students to learn from and rely upon the experts in their respective academic domains. In addition, they also want to teach students to become experts themselves who are independent critical thinkers in their field, with the knowledge and skill to then critique other experts.

Yet, when it comes to the moral domain—throughout history—higher education has gradually and increasingly shirked a responsibility to help students become moral experts in life. Instead of trying to set forth a moral vision or set of visions of a good person—or even what it might mean to be a good neighbor, friend, family member, steward of culture, caretaker of the environment and more—institutions have limited any moral expertise they claim to provide students to teaching what it means to be an excellent student, professional, and/or citizen.[4]

Stanley Fish recently produced the most radical reducing approach. He maintained, "It is the professional, and in some sense moral, obligation of faculty members to check their moral commitments at the door."[5] Fish's normative claim was based on his one primary moral identity—the professional identity of the faculty. He argued that universities and the professors employed by them should not offer answers to moral questions or shape students' character in accord with some larger vision of the good beyond a vision associated with what it means to be excellent in one's professional identity. In other words, he believed the university should only promote a specific moral vision, rooted in a student's vocational identity and the university's limited vocational mission.

Thus, Fish was still morally demanding of universities and their expectations of students. He still insisted that universities must take moral stands on issues such as "the integrity of scholarship, the evil of plagiarism, the value of liberal education."[6] He also believed that moral training involves promoting particular intellectual virtues such as "thoroughness, perseverance, [and] intellectual honesty."[7] In this respect, Fish's approach is quite compatible with efforts to promote and teach professional ethics across the disciplines.[8]

Fish did not think, however, that professors teaching professional ethics courses, such as business, communication, or engineering ethics, should defend certain moral views on controversial issues. "Analyzing ethical issues is one thing, deciding them is another, and only the first is an appropriate academic activity."[9] Thus, even discovering and discussing what it means to be a good engineer, journalist, or scientist in controversial moral situations, in Fish's view, should be limited to exploring options and not reaching conclusions.

The vast majority of professors and universities have not gone as far as Fish. Instead, they have resorted to making the identity of citizenship their primarily moral identity for moral position taking in the university. Thus, they claim to offer students moral expertise, not only regarding what it means to be a good professional, but also what it means to be a good citizen.

Unfortunately, they also end up turning the liberal democratic moral tradition into a kind of secular religion. In my recent volume, *The Dismantling of Moral Education*, I called this religion Meta-Democracy. Meta-Democracy, particularly as articulated by John Dewey and an emerging group of political thinkers, was and still is characterized by a number of important traits:

1. Educational institutions are expected to inculcate a belief in liberal democracy.
2. Autonomy and justice should be the moral ends and not simply means to moral ends.
3. The liberal defense of minority rights as a key facet of the American moral framework, while important, needs to be supplemented (and in some cases replaced) with the inculcation of justice, autonomy, and beneficence as the most important and preeminent moral virtues.[10]

The one trait tying everything together is the promotion of the emerging democratic moral tradition as the primary justification for moral education.[11]

According to faculty and universities guided by Meta-Democracy, moral expertise ultimately involves choosing a life dedicated to the broad moral principles of justice, autonomy, and beneficence/caring. It is the way students *ought* to develop, particularly in a liberal democracy. Thus, self-authorship involves building a set of moral principles that are self-chosen, because the best democratic citizen is an autonomous chooser of the good life. Yet, everyone who reasons properly will eventually choose to reason and live according to principles upon which we can all agree (i.e., justice and caring).

To this end, I prefer to call the self-authored vision of the student the Ideal Democratized Self because of its resemblance to Alasdair MacIntyre's description of such a self. Of this self, MacIntyre writes, "This democratized self which has no necessary social content and no necessary social identity can then be anything, can assume any role or take any point of view, because it is in and for itself nothing."[12]

Without any essential identity, one simply uses autonomous moral reasoning to judge whether some moral principles or virtues are better than others. Without sources of moral wisdom, one is left with the emotivist self that chooses those virtues based on simple personal preference, once again, detached from any "external" worldview, metanarrative, or guiding framework placing more weight on certain virtues than others. MacIntyre argues that this emotivist self has "an abstract and ghostly quality" when compared to other visions of the self.[13]

In addition to leading to emotivism, the Democratized Self is problematic because it necessarily requires a deficit model of moral development. According to this model, previous social (e.g., familial, ethnic, etc.) or transcendent (e.g., religious, philosophical) identities and other people, groups, or beings associated with those identities are not understood as areas of moral expertise that need to be developed. Instead, they are understood *primarily* as possible threats to the moral self-authorship necessary for autonomous democratic citizens instead of possible sources of moral wisdom and accountability.

In fact, one well-known higher education theorist, Vincent Tinto, claimed, "In order to become fully incorporated in the life of the college, individuals have to physically as well as socially dissociate themselves from the communities of the past."[14] This disassociation involved the moral domain, since "such communities differ from college not only in composition but also in the values, norms, and behavioral and intellectual styles that characterize their everyday life. As a result, the process leading to the adoption of behaviors and norms appropriate to the life of the college necessarily requires some degree of transformation and perhaps rejection of the norms of past communities."[15]

Not surprisingly, there is evidence that this approach leaves students short-changed when it comes to moral expertise. For example, Christian Smith and his fellow researchers found that the majority of college-aged emerging adults do not have the conceptual skills necessary for identifying a moral dilemma. They attributed this view to "an anemic view of what even counts in emerging adult life as moral or as concerning morality."[16] These young adults simply failed to see the moral dimension of their decisions in all the different facets of their lives. They observed, "Much of life seems to them to be a neutral zone, in which moral goods and bads are absent or irrelevant."[17] These young people could not even think in moral categories when prompted.

Furthermore, Smith and his researchers also exposed a second deficiency related to emerging adults' moral reasoning about larger ethical matters. To possess some degree of moral expertise, one must be informed of the various moral traditions and understand their implications. This knowledge would be essential to what could be called a liberal arts education in ethics.

Yet, Smith and his team determined that "most do not appeal to a moral philosophy, tradition, or ethic as an external guide by which to think and live in moral terms. Few emerging adults even seem aware that such external, coherent approaches or resources for moral reasoning exist."[18] In other words, these emerging adults either had not been educated about the historical range of moral philosophies and traditions, or they did not know how to draw upon them when actually asked to engage in moral reasoning.

Smith and his team viewed this problem as an educational failure on the part of adults. At the end of their analysis, they mince no words. They contended, "We remain concerned that the thinking expressed not only reflects what must have been a very poor moral education and formation, but it is also unable to result in good moral decision making and a morally coherent life."[19]

In the end, they concluded, "The adult world that has socialized these youth for 18 to 23 years has done an awful job when it comes to moral education and formation," and especially noted, "Colleges and universities appear to be playing a part in this failure as well."[20] As a result, they concluded the young emerging adults they interviewed are "a generation that has been failed, when it comes to moral formation."[21] What would solve this problem? Smith and his research team suggested that students "need some better moral maps and better-equipped guides to show them the way around. The question is, do those maps and guides exist, and can they be put into use?"[22]

This book introduces a different way of thinking about moral education in both the curricular and cocurricular spheres that involves introducing students to these maps and mentors. This approach proposes giving students the moral education tools by which to understand the moral identity conflicts going on around them and to help them think creatively about the discovery, construction, and prioritization of their own identities.

This approach relies upon other traditions of moral development rooted in thick understandings of human flourishing. These communities encourage broader forms of moral expertise that range across all of one's life. These thicker forms of expertise require the development of a moral identity that involves multiple facets of the moral life—a guiding purpose and conception of the good life, clear virtues and vices, mentors and models, and practices. It contends that moral expertise is acquired in ways similar to intellectual, athletic, artistic, or musical expertise: within communities of focused mentors and participants engaging in practice to acquire virtues to reach moral purposes.

DEFINING MORAL EXPERTISE

What do I mean by moral expertise? I choose to focus on moral expertise over the common term, moral development, because it emphasizes the role that humans play in shaping someone to an ideal end. In fact, I will argue that the new science of expertise can likely teach us more than some of the old approach to moral development.[23] Older scholarship on moral development often gets bogged down in debates about whether moral development is primarily a cognitive, intuitive, affective, or behavioral matter.[24] The new science of expertise, when applied to moral issues, acknowledges those issues, but it helps us move beyond them.

I do not mean to say that there have not been prior scholarly conversations about what it means to be a moral expert. Yet, the dominant view in this older conversation has been that a moral expert is an expert moral reasoner and chooser or "more capable of critically thinking through the nature of moral problems."[25] As such, a moral expert is adept in judging correctly on a moral issue and communicating that judgment well to others.

In contrast, the more expansive view of moral expertise used in this volume is that it is "not simply a matter of skill in moral reasoning and judgment. Character, conduct, and consequences are also important and, in some ways, more basic."[26] Moral expertise involves acquiring the capacities and character to live the good life.

AUDIENCE

The audience for this volume is primarily those educators and students who inhabit the culture of contemporary American higher education. In other words, I am writing this book for virtually every educator, student life staff member, and student. Of course, it will be of particular interest to higher education faculty and staff who deal directly with the moral lives of students. Eric Ericson argued in his 1968 work, *Identity, Youth and Crisis*, that at that time there was a "relative waning of the parents and the emergence of young adult specialist as the permanent and permanently changing authority" in a young adult's life.[27]

This change, he maintained, meant that the professional classes overseeing youth development should take increasing responsibility "for the orientation of the specialists and of older youth."[28] Furthermore, there was one vital aspect of this orientation. This education, he maintained, "we can only do by recognizing and cultivating an age-specific *ethical* capacity in older youth—which is the true criterion of identity."[29] What exactly this has meant and what it might mean in the future is one of the subjects of this book.

THE ROAD MAP OF THE BOOK

Scholarly resources for more expansive approaches to moral education on college campuses exist. This book draws upon these resources from across the disciplines to set forth a new interdisciplinary vision for moral education in American higher education.

The book is divided into three parts. Part I considers how three different disciplines help us understand the relationship between moral excellence and identity. Chapter 1 draws upon philosophy and sociology to establish why identity is so important to ethics. The chapter both defines identity and describes how it provides the basis for overcoming what philosophers have described as the "is-ought" gap—how one moves from descriptive accounts of identity to a normative account of what humans ought to do. Then, the chapter teases apart the essential elements of what it means to be excellent in an identity, drawing upon the discipline of sociology to illuminate the process by which we socialize students into identity excellence.

Yet, socializing students into moral traditions is never the overall end of moral education. To be effective, students must internalize these traditions as part of their own moral identity. Chapter 2 describes the burgeoning social and psychological understanding of identity transmission and the importance of developing a moral identity for producing moral motivation and moral ownership within students.

Finally, chapter 3 explores the sociological and philosophical complications that emerge when seeking to educate students for multiple forms of identity excellence in multiple identities. It points out that, although humans have built moral traditions that attempt to answer both what it means to be excellent in particular identities and what it means to be an excellent human being as a whole, various theories of identity development fail to take these traditions into account. The end of this chapter presents the case for a broad theological tradition rooted in the functional view that humans are made in God's image.

Part II applies these frames to analyze contemporary moral education in higher education. To start, chapter 4 builds the case that general education has failed to address the importance of identity excellence, in particular, and moral education, in general. As a result, students both dislike general education and fail to encounter any significant moral substance within it.

Chapter 5 then discusses how moral education in the curriculum of the contemporary university has largely been reduced to identity excellence in one's particular profession or major. The result has been a major reduction of the identity spheres that higher education addresses in the curriculum. Consequently, the other spheres are largely left to be addressed in the cocurricular dimension of the university.

Unfortunately, as chapter 6 demonstrates, cocurricular educators have largely reduced moral education to that of being a good citizen. Guided by the narrative of Meta-Democracy, such a reduction means that important dimensions of students' moral lives are totally neglected.

Part III sets forth a vision for correcting the above problems by pursuing human flourishing through identity excellence. Chapter 7 starts by doing one of the most wasteful, stupidest, idiotic things you can do in higher education. In it, I make a case for changing general education, even suggesting we abolish general education as it currently exists in most institutions. The chapter explores how effective pedagogy starts with a key question that is most *relevant* to the student. In this case, the question is, "Who am I?" This question proves challenging for students navigating—sometimes for the first time—many identities. In response, the chapter explores what it means to help students navigate and steward—morally—their Great Identities. It also outlines how we can teach the moral conversation about what it means to be excellent in the Great Identities.

Once students understand the moral elements of an identity role and what it means to be excellent in the Great Identities, they can better understand moral conflict. One of the major ways moral conflict occurs is when the moral elements of one of our identities clashes with the moral elements of another identity. In fact, it is in this pursuit of identity excellence that moral conflict usually occurs and learning to order one's identities is fundamental to resolving these moral conflicts. Thus, chapter 8 explores how we can help students think about identity prioritization and integration.

Finally, the conclusion sets forth the argument that the ultimate resolution of these moral conflicts can only be accomplished through what I call the theological frame. When students are taught to understand themselves as humans made in God's image, they acquire an overarching telos that not only helps them order their identities, but also helps enrich these identities. Rather than diminishing their identities, students contribute the very best of themselves in pursuit of the greatest degree of human flourishing.

NOTES

1. Lawrence Kohlberg, *The Philosophy of Moral Development: Moral Stages and the Idea of Justice, Essays on Moral Development* (San Francisco: Harper and Row, 1981), 1:143.

2. Philippa Foot, "The Problem of Abortion and the Doctrine of the Double Effect," *Oxford Review*, 5 (1967): 5–15.

3. Dean Holland, dir., *The Good Place*, season 2, episode 5, "The Trolley Problem," aired October 19, 2017 on NBC.

4. Perry L. Glanzer, *The Dismantling of Moral Education: How Higher Education Reduced the Human Identity* (Lanham, MD: Rowman & Littlefield, 2022).

5. Stanley Fish, "The Case for Academic Autonomy," *The Chronicle of Higher Education*, July 23, 2004, 1. For his more extended argument see Stanley Fish, *Save the World on Your Own Time* (New York: Oxford University Press, 2008).

6. Fish, *Save the World on Your Own Time*, 19.

7. Fish, *Save the World on Your Own Time*, 20.

8. Michael Davis, *Ethics and the University* (New York: Routledge, 1999).

9. Michael Davis, *Ethics and the University*, 27.

10. William Frankena famously argued that justice and beneficence comprise moral excellence. William Frankena, *Ethics*, 2nd ed. (Englewood Cliffs, NJ: Prentice Hall, 1973).

11. See for example Jeffrey Stout, *Democracy and Tradition* (Princeton, NJ: Princeton University Press, 2004) and Anne Colby, Thomas Ehrlich, Elizabeth Beaumont, Jason Stephens, *Educating Citizens: Preparing America's Undergraduates for Lives of Moral and Civic Responsibility* (San Francisco: Jossey-Bass, 2003).

12. Alasdair MacIntyre, *After Virtue*, 3rd ed. (South Bend: University of Notre Dame Press, 2007), 37.

13. MacIntyre, *After Virtue*, 38.

14. Vincent Tinto, *Leaving College: Rethinking the Causes and Cures of Student Attrition*, 2nd ed. (Chicago: University of Chicago Press, 1993), 96.

15. Tinto, *Leaving College*, 95–96.

16. Christian Smith with Kari M. Hojara, Hilary A. Davidson, and Patricia Snell Herzog, *Lost in Transition: The Dark Side of Emerging Adulthood* (New York: Oxford University Press, 2011), 65.

17. Smith et al., *Lost in Transition*, 65.

18. Smith et al., *Lost in Transition*, 26.

19. Smith et al., *Lost in Transition*, 31.

20. Smith et al., *Lost in Transition*, 60, 61.

21. Smith et al., *Lost in Transition*, 69.

22. Smith et al., *Lost in Transition*, 69.

23. Anders Ericsson and Robert Pool, *Peak: Secrets from the New Science of Expertise* (New York: Houghton Mifflin Harcourt, 2016).

24. John C. Gibbs, *Moral Development and Reality: Beyond the Theories of Kohlberg, Hoffman, and Haidt*, 4th ed. (New York: Oxford University Press, 2019).

25. John Woods and Douglas Walton, "Moral Expertise," *Journal of Moral Education* 5, no. 1 (1975): 13; see also Lawrence Kohlberg, *The Philosophy of Moral Development: Moral Stages and the Idea of Justice, Essays on Moral Development, Vol. 1* (San Francisco: Harper and Row Publishers, 1981); William G. Perry Jr., *Forms of Intellectual and Ethical Development in the College Years: A Scheme* (San Francisco: Jossey-Bass, 1999/1968).

26. Peter Miller, "Who are the Moral Experts?" *Journal of Moral Education* 5, no. 1 (1975): 4.

27. Erik H. Erikson, *Identity, Youth and Crisis* (New York: W. W. Norton & Company, 1968), 39.

28. Erikson, *Identity, Youth and Crisis*, 39.

29. Erikson, *Identity, Youth and Crisis*, 39.

PART I

Understanding the Relationship between Moral Excellence and Identity

By definition and mission statement, naturalistic scientism cannot recognize much less adequately understand and account for, immaterial realities, like value, meaning, morality, and personhood. So it is stuck with the misguided task of denying, reducing, eliminating, and explaining away, with terms alien to the realities themselves, that which is often most important in human life.

—Christian Smith[1]

To state the obvious, Serena Williams and Louis Armstrong did not achieve excellence in tennis and trumpet playing, respectively, simply through natural development. Certainly, their natural development played a role in their achievement of excellence (and with Serena Williams will play a role in her decline), but achieving excellence involves a range of other factors. These include personal motivation, deliberate practice under mentors and coaches to acquire habitual virtues, a community of practice, and more. These factors are common to others who achieve excellence.[2]

Despite these obvious characteristics about the nature of excellence in other fields, certain romantics throughout history have thought that moral excellence is different. According to Jean-Jacques Rousseau's *Emile*, for example, we should allow young people to develop morally in nonhuman nature and away from corrupting human society. It could even be argued that Edgar Rice Burroughs's Tarzan was a popular expression of Rousseau's ideals.

Not surprisingly, Rousseau never raised his own children, but instead had his mistress take those he sired to an orphanage.[3] Spending time away from created human culture offers much, but as William Golding, the author of *The Lord of the Flies*, knew all too well, achieving moral excellence is not a natural product of such experiences. Instead, the jungle can become the playground for those with power, made all too evident as Burroughs' racism filtered through his books. Moral excellence is not developed "naturally," unless the nature referenced includes humans and human society and culture.

Human moral excellence, like other forms of human excellence, requires learning to do things so that they become "second nature." We should recognize that we do not just evolutionarily fall into, or naturally develop, the good. We must discover it, choose it, and then engage in the hard work of making it become second nature.

Unfortunately, academia has endured an odd quest for the past five hundred years in which natural scientists presume to provide insight into how to discover the good and achieve it. As James Davison Hunter and Paul Nedelisky have demonstrated in *Science and the Good: The Tragic Quest for the Foundations of Morality*, the attempt to use science to fulfill the quest for the human good has failed:

> When it began, the quest for moral science sought to discover the good. The new moral science has abandoned that quest and now, at best, tells us how to get what we want. With this turn, the new moral science, for all its recent fanfare, has produced a world picture that simply cannot bear the weight of the wide-ranging moral burdens of our time.[4]

To correct this weakness with science, Hunter and Nedelisky helpfully outline three possible ways science could provide answers in the moral realm:

> The most interesting way—always the highest aspiration of those who have sought a scientific foundation for morality—would be if science could settle longstanding moral questions. Call this level of scientific results "Level One."
>
> "Level Two" findings, while falling short of demonstrating some moral doctrine, would still give evidence for or against some moral claim or theory. For instance, if there was empirical evidence that virtue theories of ethics were false, but the evidence fell short of settling that this or that moral claim was correct.
>
> "Level Three" findings would provide scientifically based descriptions of, say, the origins of morality, or the specific way our capacity for moral judgment is physically embodied in our neural architecture, or whether human beings tend to behave in ways we consider moral.[5]

Hunter and Nedelisky go on to observe that no scientists claim to offer Level One findings. Level Two claims are sparse. Thus, almost all the supposed scientific findings about morality over the last five hundred years are at Level Three. They conclude,

> The most recent science has provided insight into the nonevaluative elements of morality and offered suggestive possibilities about its claims on human experience. But it has given us nothing remotely close to an empirical foundation for morality—nothing close to an "ought" from an "is."[6]

As they point out, one of the core problems is the failure to start with clear definitions.

Philosophy, which has been dealing with these matters for thousands of years, provides a better place to start when it comes to matters of definitions. Chapter 1 defines and overviews a set of key moral concepts that we need in order to understand the pursuit if identity excellence.

Yet, one of the problems with our conversations about moral excellence, moral education, and identity is that the conversation also takes place across multiple different disciplines that have important insights to add. As a result, in chapters 2 and 3, important insights from sociology, psychology, and theology are added to the mix to set forth the groundwork for an interdisciplinary basis for a vision of Identity Excellence.

NOTES

1. Christian Smith, *What is a Person?* (Chicago: University of Chicago Press, 2010), 114.

2. Anders Ericsson and Robert Pool, *Peak: Secrets from the New Science of Expertise* (New York: Houghton Mifflin Harcourt, 2016).

3. Paul Johnson, *Intellectuals* (New York: Harper & Row, 1988).

4. James Davison Hunter and Paul Nedelisky, *Science and the Good: The Tragic Quest for the Foundations of Morality* (New Haven, CT: Yale University Press, 2019), xv.

5. Hunter and Nedelisky, *Science and the Good*, 99–100.

6. Hunter and Nedelisky, *Science and the Good*, 139.

Chapter 1

Who Am I and Who Should I Become?

Philosophical and Sociological Frames

Interviewer: "What do you think is the purpose of higher education?"
University senior: "I think it's also about finding yourself, who you want
  to be, what you believe, and just finding your identity."

To pursue moral excellence and gain moral expertise, the most important
initial questions a person needs to answer are not, "What do I do in a moral
dilemma? How complicated is my moral reasoning? How successful is my
virtue acquisition?" Instead, the most important question is: "Who am I?" The
philosopher Charles Taylor observed, "To know who you are is to be oriented
in moral space, a space in which questions arise about what is good or bad,
what is worth doing and what is not, what has meaning and importance for
you and what is trivial and secondary."[1] Taylor later asserts, "Our identity is
what allows us to define what is important to us and what is not."[2]

To understand Taylor's point, some important clarifications and increased
specificity are needed. Thus, this chapter will first clarify the definition of the
term "identity" used in this volume before drawing upon recent philosophical
literature to clarify why identity is important for ethics. Finally, it will explain
the important moral dimensions needed to understand and talk about identity
excellence and moral expertise.

DEFINITIONS

Throughout this book, the term "identity" refers to one of two different
meanings delineated in dictionary definitions. It comes from the second
Oxford English Dictionary definition that contains two parts. The first part,

2a, defines identity as: "The sameness of a person or thing at all times or in all circumstances; the condition of being a single individual; the fact that a person or thing is itself and not something else; individuality, personality."[3] For example, there is only one Perry Glanzer in the world (and indeed according to Google there is only one). Someone may steal my identity, but I am the only Perry Glanzer who has some essential identity that stays the same through time. Of course, many students, when testifying before an honor council, often try to get around this reality by claiming, "It really is not me," when trying to explain their dishonest behavior.

The second part, 2b, states: "Who or what a person or thing is; a distinct impression of a single person or thing presented to or perceived by others; a set of characteristics or a description that distinguishes a person or thing from others." For instance, Perry Glanzer is also a husband, father, professor, American citizen, male, friend, one-half Austrian, one-eighth Dutch, one-eighth German, and one-quarter Norwegian, a neighbor, a steward of my body, a caretaker of the natural world, and more.

Today, the emphasis upon understanding this kind of identity has less to do with these short identity words and more to do with the narratives associated with all these identity words. Thus, our identities are understood as less related to the first definition of identity mentioned above and more related to the definitions of identity in the latter two identities.

In this respect, it matters less that I am half Austrian and more that my ancestors were imprisoned and then evicted from Austria by the Hapsburgs because they were Mennonite pacifists. Next, they were evicted from Romania for the same reason. They fled to Russia (present-day Ukraine) and lived there for some time, but in the 1870s they were asked to fight in the czar's wars. At that point they decided to come to America for religious freedom. Thus, for many scholars our personal stories and the stories of our groups are what really comprise identity.[4]

Even so, I will be using both understandings of identity throughout this book. Part of the argument is that the most important thing we can do is "know thyself" and study these various forms of identity, which indeed are quite complicated. For instance, I once told a group of Texan adults that I was teaching, that I was half Texan and half Coloradan (besides four-year stints in Iowa and California, I had lived in both Colorado and Texas the same amount of time). I heard a murmur from the crowd and one man yelled out, "You can't be half Texan!" This example is just one such complication as we think about how others believe our different identities can and should combine. Another complication is that though we are born with some of these identities, we can also gain and lose some. I am always a son, but I was not always a father. I was a student but now I am a professor. Knowing thyself becomes complicated.

WHY IDENTITIES ARE SO IMPORTANT IN ETHICS

Identities are the key to ethics in three particular ways. First, they are the solution to what philosophers call the "is-ought" gap or the "naturalistic fallacy." The earlier purveyors of this fallacy maintained that one cannot derive a moral or evaluative conclusion (an "ought") from factual premises (an "is").

In *After Virtue*, however, Alasdair MacIntyre demonstrates that this supposedly uncrossable is-ought gap, actually, is crossed successfully when we pinpoint a person's identity and then ask how we determine whether someone is a good or excellent [fill in the identity blank]. As a result, he points out, "From such factual premises as 'He gets a better yield for this crop per acre than any farmer in the district,' 'He has the most effective programme of soil renewal yet known' and 'His dairy herd wins all the first prizes at the agricultural shows,' the evaluative conclusion validly follows that 'He is a good farmer.'"[5]

In other words, our identities are almost always associated with traditions of excellence related to that identity. Of course, as anyone who has served on a tenure committee knows, this fact does not mean we do not argue about what should comprise that tradition of excellence or expertise.

There is a second reason why identities are so important to ethics. Identities expand and limit the scope of our moral obligations. When one becomes a spouse or a parent, one takes upon moral obligations to one's spouse or children that one does not have toward other spouses or children. In addition, one hopefully undertakes the pursuit of moral excellence in these identities. So, how does one then obtain moral excellence in an identity? Although certainly each identity is different, the discipline of ethics helps us understand some categorically similar features associated with obtaining excellence in each identity.[6]

Finally, as will be discussed further in chapter 3, we have multiple identities with multiple traditions of identity excellence that we must learn to prioritize and/or integrate. First, however, we need to examine what comprises moral excellence in one's identity.

IDENTIFYING THE ELEMENTS OF MORAL EXCELLENCE IN AN IDENTITY

To begin, as noted in the introduction, students first need two cognitive assets to pursue identity excellence—a moral vocabulary and a basic moral map to guide their way. To be clear, acquiring these assets does not require moral educators to tell students what to do or where to go on the moral map of life, something ethicists generally avoid (as wonderfully portrayed in the character of Chidi in *The Good Place*). That said, moral educators do need to help students recognize and understand the moral dimension present in everything they do. Humans live in "moral space," and part of their task is to acquire their bearings within the moral realm.[7] Thus, moral excellence is inherent to daily life rather than simply being about rare decisions found in difficult case studies of ethics textbooks.

What helps someone get their moral bearings and think within a moral framework? Young children receive their moral bearings from their conscience, parents, teachers, and other important adults in their lives. Throughout the K–12 period, the role of parents and moral and intellectual educators and mentors in particular involves helping children know the good, love the good, and do the good.[8] During this time, students' sense of self is usually underdeveloped and disconnected from the moral orientation they receive.[9]

At this time, it makes sense to help students develop moral expertise in the same way we help children develop expertise in other dimensions of life. We introduce them to generally agreed-upon standards about what it means to be excellent in particular identities (e.g., a good student, a good friend, a good caretaker of the environment, etc.). Children—and often even college students—need to be taught to think, feel, and act in light of these moral categories. What are these categories?

Knowing the good, or identity excellence, requires a knowledge of the moral components of an identity and the journey toward identity excellence (as defined in this volume). To help students uncover the moral elements, it helps to ask them to consider what it might mean to be excellent in a performance identity role of their choice, such as being a good basketball player, as well as a morally-charged identity role, such as being a good husband or wife (the new word "partner" carries little historical moral tradition with it and is not as morally helpful).[10]

Students can identify several elements, but are rarely able to identify all nine moral elements that they need to consider to "know the good" of a particular identity. Therefore, the rest of this chapter categorizes and briefly presents the essential elements that have been delineated by various philosophers. The key components of identity excellence are:

1. Narrative
2. Purposes/Ends
3. Rules
4. Virtues
5. Practices
6. Wisdom
7. Mentors

8. Moral Imagination
9. Models, Exemplars, Heroes, or Saints

Narrative, Purposes/Ends, and Rules

How best do we know certain identities? Our identity knowledge is not something we simply individually create or, to use the term popular in student affairs today, we "self-author." After all, as I discuss more extensively in chapter 2, we have to use the language and resources of our various prior moral cultures to understand ourselves. Willem Wardekker and Siebren Miedema explain, "Individual stories are created through the use of story schemata, genres, motives, metaphors, examples, and other elements that are found in culture. (It is exactly the use of such cultural elements that makes an individual's story comprehensible to others and to the self.) Moreover, other people play a role in the construction process: as audience, as people to relate the story to, as co-constructors."[11] As Wardekker and Miedema make clear, according to this view, one cannot even make or retell individual stories without reference to the social relationships and schema that culture provides, and others understand. Thus, understanding identity—and various identities, at that—is a complex endeavor that acknowledges that identities do not exist within a vacuum. Consequently, we consider the roles that narrative, purposes, and rules play in shaping identity.

First, individuals primarily understand their individual and collective identities in the form of *narratives*. Although one's individual or communal identity may be connected to certain practices (e.g., being Norwegian and eating lutefisk), there is much more to the identity than simple practices. In other words, whether it is one's personal name (e.g., Mary), family name (e.g., Doe), one's ethnic identity, national identity, gender, religious/nonreligious identity, professional identity, family identity, or another form of identity, each unique aspect of identity has stories attached. For instance, the short story regarding my one-eighth Dutch and one-eighth German identity is that my German great-great grandmother lived near the border of the Netherlands and married a Dutch builder. They were fairly well-to-do, but he started drinking, lost most of their money, and started abusing the family. So, my great-great-grandmother fled to the United States as a single mother with her seven children ages three to sixteen to live with her brother.

One of the predominant ways we understand what it means to be an American, for example, concerns not only the ideas in the United States Constitution, but also our conversations and disagreements about what those ideas mean in practice. Through narratives about these struggles, and sometimes even competing narratives, we make sense of this identity, and in similar ways, other identities.[12] One's personal struggle both to understand these identities and order any ethical demands associated with them will entail affective struggles.

Yet, even when people encounter tensions or discomfort regarding some portion of their identity, they often relate how they resolved these tensions in the form of a personal or communal narrative.[13] For example, in order to understand how I came to terms with my Texas identity, you would have to listen to my story about being uprooted from beautiful Colorado in seventh grade, moving to Texas and hating it for two years, and then slowly coming to appreciate certain parts of its culture, story, and mindset (especially its friend-liness, emphasis upon relationships, and hospitality), while at the same time still rejecting parts of that story (e.g., racism and distrust of outsiders). In this narrative form, identity is perhaps best summarized by Christian Smith, who defines identities as "self-understandings derived from occupying particular stable locations in social, behavioral, mental and moral space that securely define who and what somebody is, for themselves and for others."[14]

Second, we must consider *ends or purposes* when examining our identi-ties. Functionally, as mentioned in the introduction, a purpose allows us to reason from what "is" to what we "ought" to do. Thus, how one understands the purpose of an identity (its ultimate function) makes a tremendous differ-ence in how one understands other key parts of the moral world related to that identity. What is the difference between the Harlem Globetrotters and the San Antonio Spurs? One plays for entertainment and the other plays to win an NBA championship.

Marriage provides another great example. How one views the purpose of marriage will necessarily influence how one determines if that marriage is healthy and successful. When I ask my students the purpose of marriage, they often offer rather one-dimensional views such as "marriage is for happi-ness" or "marriage is for personal joy."[15] Nevertheless, these purposes fail to account for the robust philosophical and religious traditions that provide the complexity needed to evaluate such a storied institution of modern life. The purposes one associates with their various identities matter and will deter-mine the trajectory of how one lives those identities out.

Third, we need to figure out the *rules* guiding our understanding of iden-tity excellence. A person cannot play an identity game without knowing the rules. In basketball, the player cannot double dribble, walk without drib-bling, kick the ball, etc. Is "Thou shalt not commit adultery" still one of the rules or should the rules committee rewrite that one? Who writes the rules and enforces them? Is it God, nature, state, or a group in civil society (e.g., church, mosque, or synagogue)? In my experience, students tend to think of the state as the primary arbiter of moral rules, thereby neglecting other sources, such as the reality of nature, God, or other communities as potential rule makers. Moral educators need to help students understand the range of possibilities for rule sets, rule makers, and rule enforcers.

I will further clarify the inherent complexity—and the need for dialogue— surrounding rules and rule writers using basketball and marriage as examples. Rules usually relate to some understanding of whether the person has the physical capabilities to join in the game. We let young children play basketball, but we do not let them marry, and at what age they can marry varies according to country. How many people can play on a team in basketball or be given to one another in marriage? The numbers always depend upon the rule makers.

Of course, the rule makers must consider physical and mental capabilities (or if the rule maker is "nature, those things are already part of nature's rules"). There is always a point at which the state will or will not allow a mentally handicapped person to marry. A person in a coma or with Alzheimer's cannot play basketball (perhaps in the early stages of Alzheimer's they can), but they can still be married. Yet even this issue is sometimes up for debate. Pat Robertson caused a stir some time ago when he mentioned that he thought divorce could be an option when facing a spouse with Alzheimer's—a striking contrast to the practice we found in the popular movie *The Notebook*, where a husband cares for a wife with dementia. Is an individual still married if she suffers from dementia? Awareness of the rules by which we are—or ought— to be playing, is crucial to understanding excellence within an identity.

Developing Virtues through Practice under Wise Mentors

Fourth and fifth, within the context of a given purpose and a set of rules, we then learn to develop the particular *virtues* of the game through habituated *practice* so that they become second nature. This idea is as old as Aristotle. No one is born being able to dribble and shoot a ball in basketball. You must learn those skills so that you can do them without thinking about them and they become second nature. In marriage, virtues we usually associate as essential for marriage—love, cherishing, humility, patience, and faithfulness—require a similar form of habituated practice. It is important to note that one must still make a cognitive choice to develop and continually nourish these virtues through practice.

Virtues, however, are not inherent to a given identity since the acquisition of virtues varies according to the purpose of the practice. Spinning a basketball on one finger is a habit acquired by practice for a Harlem Globetrotter, but it is not a valuable habit for NBA players. This is the reason why Kohlberg criticized the "bag of virtues" approach.[16] People set forth different virtues for the same identity and its excellence because they have different understandings of the ultimate function or purpose of that identity. The problem is further exacerbated when there is disagreement about the purpose of life as a whole.

Without such agreement, it is unlikely that there will be agreement about the virtues necessary for the flourishing of a particular role, let alone life as a whole. One could think the purpose of marriage is to maximize one's pleasure, to provide economic stability, to establish spiritual union and formation, to raise children for the state, or something else. Each of these different purposes will influence the virtues a person deems necessary for a successful marriage.

Recently, to categorize different types of virtues, the philosopher Jason Baehr made a distinction between intellectual, moral, civic, and performance virtues.[17] Baehr differentiated his categorization of virtues by to whom they are ascribed: intellectual virtue is the virtue of the good thinker or learner, moral virtue is the virtue of a good neighbor, and civic virtue is the virtue of a good citizen. In other words, particular virtues are connected to specific identities, and Baehr himself admits that we may need more categories for virtue beyond what he offers.[18]

To extend Baehr's argument, I contend that virtue is always defined and informed by a person's partial identities (e.g., the virtues associated with being a good student/scholar, a good family member, a good friend, a good neighbor, a good citizen, a good steward of nature, a good student of culture, a good steward of one's race, a good Texan, etc.), as well as larger identities and narratives that may define and shape one's whole identity (e.g., a human being made in God's image who finds human flourishing by imitating God's virtues).

Understanding this point also helps us make sense of moral conflict. When identity conflicts occur among virtues, each person must recognize and choose a particular metaidentity, metanarrative, and set of metavirtues that will be prioritized over others (e.g., for certain individuals the performance virtues necessary to be an Olympic champion may be tempered by the moral virtue of love in all of one's identities).

Discussing virtues in terms of the myriad of human identities and not simply four categories is ideal because it accounts for the multidimensional nature of virtue and our relationships. For example, being a good caretaker of nature involves all kinds of relational dimensions and associated virtues between a person and themselves (caring for one's own body by showing self-control); a person and earth (caring for nature using one's wisdom); a person and others living today and in the future (caring for nature by using intellectual curiosity and innovation within an intellectual community); and perhaps a person and God (caring for God's creation through faithfulness, gratitude, love, etc.).

In addition, we must recognize that not all types of practice to develop virtues are the same. In Anders Ericsson's research on experts, he noted that there are three different types of practice. First, there is what Ericsson calls "naive practice" in which a person does something over and over again in the hopes that they will get better. He gives a sample conversation between a music teacher and a student:

TEACHER: Your practice sheet says that you practice an hour a day, but your playing test was only a C. Can you explain why?
STUDENT: I don't know what happened! I could play the test last night!
TEACHER: How many times did you play it?
STUDENT: Ten or twenty.
TEACHER: How many times did you play it correctly?
STUDENT: Umm, I dunno. . . . Once or twice.
TEACHER: Hmm. . . . How did you practice it?
STUDENT: I dunno. I just played it.[19]

Ericsson calls the second type of practice "purposeful practice." This kind of practice has four key elements: 1) it has well-defined, specific goals, 2) it is focused, 3) it involves feedback, and 4) it requires getting out of one's comfort zone.[20]

An example of a teacher encouraging the first element in the scenario above would be, "Play the piece all the way through at the proper speed without a mistake three times in a row."[21] For our basketball player, it might be "make three hundred 3-point shots a day from every part of the 3-point arc."

To fulfill the second element of purposeful practice, you would not seek to fulfill these goals casually. You would need to play or shoot as if in the game. My father always told me never to practice layups at a casual pace because you will rarely be doing a casual layup in an actual basketball game. Therefore, you should practice them with focus, at full speed.

In marriage, one could imagine the benefit of a similar type of focus for a spouse who has trouble with encouragement: compliment your spouse ten times a day. Furthermore, spouses must learn certain conflict-resolution virtues (e.g., self-control, kindness, forgiveness) and practices, and they must be able to practice them in the heat of an emotionally charged conflict.

The final two elements of Ericsson's deliberate practice—feedback and getting out of one's comfort zone—involve introducing the sixth and seventh elements of identity excellence. These are *wisdom* and the *coaches* who have it. Wisdom is neither rules nor behavioral virtues, but the knowledge that comes from excellent study and practice. This kind of expert knowledge is the kind acquired by someone who has observed and practiced in the field for some time. Someone who has played and observed basketball for years can often predict whether a player will make a 3-point shot or a free throw by looking at the mechanics of a shot, or whether the shot was taken after receiving a pass from a certain place on the floor and in a certain rhythm of the game.[22]

Of course, depending on the level of expertise, sometimes this advice is more mundane. When I was in tenth grade, I was playing a game of two-on-two. My partner was our 6'5" center who was guarded by my 5'10" older brother. I kept trying to feed our center using bounce passes. Bounce passes are a key virtue of the game I had learned through practice. They are also obviously not against the rules.

Yet, as my quick brother continually stole my bounce passes, my coach finally came over and told me to start feeding the ball to my playing partner at the highest point of his out-stretched arm where my brother could not reach it. This was rather simple wisdom, but I still needed to hear it, since my continual errors were making us lose the game. Under the guidance of my coach, I soon gained expertise in lob passes to our big men down low, placing the ball in the exact place that allowed them to catch the ball and shoot in one motion.

Similarly, I remember reading how Phil Jackson was coaching the Lakers during their many championship years with Kobe Bryant and Shaquille O'Neal, and how he predicted during practices whether a player would make or miss the shot based on where the pass was given to the shooter. Studies of the most successful basketball coach in college history, John Wooden, found that the majority of his instruction involved imparting this kind of wisdom.[23]

We expect coaches or mentors to possess this type of wisdom. If one examines the autobiographies of great athletes, one finds that even at the pinnacle of success in their sport, the greatest athletes in the world still needed coaches to provide them with the wisdom to perfect their practice. This wisdom is the feedback that may help a person get outside their comfort zone—thereby fulfilling Ericsson's third and fourth elements of deliberate practice. Receiving feedback is uncomfortable because it often requires us to change our habits, but when we get outside our comfort zone, we have the capacity to practice and play at another level.

The same proves true with any other human practice such as marriage, friendship, being a good citizen, or life as a whole. Marriage requires a similar type of wisdom, often gained through coaches to help with purposeful practice. This type of wisdom may involve figuring out how to love your spouse in unique ways. Does loving one's spouse mean buying flowers, showing more physical affection, taking out the trash, changing diapers, or changing the oil in their car (or perhaps all of the above)? Purposeful practice may involve breaking through a particular type of communication or conflict pattern that seems to come about no matter how often you try to avoid it. At some points, you may need a mentor or coach to help you.

What should be clear is that this kind of pursuit of deliberate practice is much different from sitting around a classroom discussing case studies of difficult moral dilemmas within one's profession. Once again, the setting or practice venue proves important.[24] Studying basketball in a classroom is not that helpful (although film study can help). Furthermore, if a basketball player who has played only on an outdoor court suddenly has to adjust to an inside arena with fans, that player's practice will have been less effective.

The same proves true for marriage. How does one practice faithfulness before marriage? What does practice look like? Is cohabitation a type of effective practice for marriage? Alternatively, is it not the same as practicing in a game situation? Does the community in which you practice marriage make a difference?

Moral Imagination

Through purposeful and deliberate practice in the virtues of the identity under a wise mentor we can gain increased *moral imagination*. Moral imagination involves two different aspects. One of the outcomes of engaging in deliberate moral practice in a specific identity is the production of particular mental representations that guide one's practice. Erikson noted, "A key fact about mental representations is that they are very domain specific . . . there is no such thing as developing a general skill."[25] The same is true with virtue. There is no such thing as general forms of honesty, love, and patience. One must learn to exercise these virtues in particular domains and identities in order to build mental representations.

These mental representations allow one to engage in a second form of moral imagination. They help you to think about doing something unique in the identity to advance excellence. Kenny Sailors invented the jump shot as a college basketball player with a certain degree of competence.[26] In marriage, one may need to imagine new ways of loving one's spouse that are not simply the common suggestions one will find in self-help books or even wisdom from a counselor. What this means is that experts are those are best positioned to promote excellence and continually develop a capacity for creativity or moral imagination.

Understood in this way, identity excellence is not simply a fixed capacity that one acquires by learning purposes, rules, virtues, practices, etc. Moral imagination creates space for one to both *be* excellent (by some contextualized/shared standard) and to *still be in pursuit* of new ways of excellence.

Models, Exemplars, Heroes, and Saints

Finally, those who have achieved excellence in the practice are those we might call *models*, *exemplars*, *heroes*, or in religious traditions, *saints*. These individuals incarnate the best of all nine elements. Young adults place posters on their walls of these models in sports such as basketball (e.g., LeBron James and Steph Curry). The following model regarding marriage comes from Peterson and Seligman's book on *Character Strengths and Virtues*. Peterson and Seligman use this story from 9/11 to illustrate the general virtue of love but notice that *virtues* such as love must be practiced in a particular identity role:

> Greg Manning could see from the terrace of his apartment that the jet had struck near the offices of Cantor Fitzgerald, where his wife worked as a senior vice president and partner. . . . He was certain that his vibrant and beautiful Lauren was dead, but he was wrong. . . . She had just entered the lobby of Tower One when a fireball descending through an elevator shaft propelled her back into the street, totally engulfed in flames. . . . At the hospital, her face swollen beyond recognition, she told Greg the pain was so excruciating she had been praying to die but then out of love for him and Tyler [their son] made the decision to fight for her life. Within a few minutes, she slipped into a drug-induced coma that would last many weeks.
>
> During his hospital shifts, Greg ignored Lauren's unconscious state, reading poetry to her, and playing her favorite CDs, all the while reassuring her that she was loved, that he would take care of her, that everything would be okay. During his home shifts, he took Tyler to birthday parties and play dates, read and sang to him, and documented his development on videotape for Lauren's future viewing. . . . Saving Lauren meant replacing more than 80% of her skin, often multiple times. . . . Exactly 3 months after admission to the hospital, Lauren saw her new, scarred face for the first time. The predictable shock and sadness were tempered by the fact that her husband had prepared her through repeated reminders that she always had been and always would be his soul mate, and in his eyes was as beautiful as ever.[27]

It is important to recognize that all the above elements work together in a modeling situation.

Love would look differently in a different role if the person were showing love as a teacher, citizen, neighbor, or parent. However, Greg's actions were informed by a larger narrative of what marital love and faithfulness involve (two unique virtues applied in a unique way in marriage), and his *purpose* in marriage was more than simply his happiness. Furthermore, Greg exemplified *wisdom* in the midst of love. One can only assume that Greg had *coaches*—be they counselors, friends, or family—to help him navigate his role as a husband, particularly during those difficult weeks.

Moreover, had he committed adultery during this time to fulfill a sexual need that was not being met, the story would not be so morally compelling, since he would have violated a *rule* of marital practice. On the contrary, Greg's ability to anticipate and respond to his wife's future needs by assuring her (in both words and actions) of his love, even as she was unable to hear him, is perhaps the most inspiring part of the story. Some may even perceive Greg's action toward his wife to be a unique embodiment of love—a compelling display of *moral imagination*. In other words, developing moral expertise and identity excellence starts by avoiding the tendency to reduce moral development to a couple moral elements (e.g., justice, empathy, etc.).

UNIVERSITIES ARE BUILT ON THE EXISTENCE AND KNOWLEDGE OF IDENTITY EXCELLENCE

In this book, I will not engage in the age-old arguments about the existence of moral knowledge related to identity excellence or how one obtains it (reasoning, intuition, habit, experience, divine revelation, etc.). I want to simply point out that universities are built on the premises that identity excellence exists, it can be discovered, and it needs to be passed along to younger generations. If any academic denies these things, they need to quit their faculty job and do something else.

Indeed, human society inescapably socializes young children into these moral elements in various identities, such as what it means to be an excellent friend, student, neighbor, parent, citizen, caretaker of earth, steward of one's body, professional, and more. We have discovered and created numerous identities in which we seek excellence, and all of those identities have the components described above.

Higher education is no different. In this understanding, the university can never avoid teaching ethics. The university teaches, informs, and supports various identities, purposes, particular rules, certain kinds of virtues and practices to achieve them, wisdom, and moral models. Silly claims about the amorality of the university originate with people who either do not understand ethical language or do not pay attention to the ethical language, socialization, and reasoning found within universities.[28] Of course, as I mentioned in the introduction, due to the moral pluralism in liberal democracies, many universities and professors do limit the identity areas where they are willing to set forth a vision of identity excellence. These limited identity areas most often include being a good professional or good citizen.

Thus, the danger is not that the university will fail to socialize students into identity excellence. Rather, the major danger is that the university will do a poor job—merely approaching the task in a haphazard, fragmented, and reductionistic way. It is not hard to find examples.

REDUCTIONISM

Some time ago, Harvard University proposed setting forth a "Freshman Pledge" that demonstrates all the problems with one-dimensional approaches to moral education. The core of the pledge stated:

> In the classroom, in extracurricular endeavors, and in the Yard and Houses, students are expected to act with integrity, respect and industry, and to sustain a community characterized by inclusiveness and civility. As we begin at Harvard, we commit to upholding the values of the College and to making the entryway and Yard a place where all can thrive and where the exercise of kindness holds a place on par with intellectual attainment.[29]

Integrity, respect, industry, civility, inclusiveness, and kindness are all worthy virtues, but the pledge did not really say why *these* virtues were particularly important over and above a host of other worthy virtues. Additionally, the pledge writers offered no definitions, neglecting to account for the many different ways of understanding these storied virtues. Will one person's honesty be another person's incivility? The pledge offers students little guidance with this critical issue.

Problematically, the Harvard Freshman Pledge provided virtues without any of the other elements necessary for thinking about what it means to be a good student and a good neighbor at Harvard. Students do not receive an explanation of the moral origins of these virtues, definitions, or readings that might explain the rich reasons for them (something that might prove helpful to a group of academe's most promising minds). Such an approach would be similar to a Catholic university asking incoming students to sign their commitment to the seven cardinal virtues without explaining their origins, what they mean, what they might look like in actual practice, or the larger purpose and metanarrative that gives them meaning and significance.

This last omission was the most serious. Only moral traditions or communities that conceptualize a specific human end—derived from particular narratives—can effectively establish rules or definitions of virtue. Based on the specific end that defines human flourishing, communities then seek to establish certain rules and embody, prioritize, and exemplify particular virtues. Yet, many higher education programs appear to seek an intellectual community devoid of a guiding tradition or narrative because such trappings prove restrictive.

In other words, instead of the Catholic university example, it might be more appropriate to say that the pledge is like asking students to learn to dribble a ball without providing them any context of the game for which such a virtue might be helpful. The Harvard Freshman Pledge had no story, no purpose, no mentors, and no saints.

Granted, Harvard College does not hope to form moral saints. Today, the first part of its pledge simply proclaims, "The mission of Harvard College is to educate the citizens and citizen-leaders for our society."[30] They only want to form students in one partial identity and not in multiple identities or the broader overarching identity of being excellent human beings. A pledge written by a committee supplies a basic civic community ritual, so perhaps it remains a small beginning to forming a slightly more vigorous moral community. Yet, bags of virtues designed to focus on community citizenship will likely be less compelling than advancing a robust moral vision of identity excellence.

Of course, society needs to pass along all these elements to the young novice seeking to be excellent in any identity (and not simply their civic identity). This knowledge will supply cognitive understanding, but it will not supply one very important element—motivation. For that we need to consider one important cognitive element, and something called moral identity.

NOTES

1. Charles Taylor, *The Sources of the Self: The Making of Modern Identity* (Cambridge, MA: Harvard University Press, 1989), 28.

2. Taylor, *The Sources of the Self*, 30.

3. *Oxford English Dictionary* (Oxford: Oxford University Press, 2000), online database.

4. See for example Susan R. and Elisa S. Abes, *Identity Development of College Students Advancing Frameworks for Multiple Dimensions of Identity*, 1st ed. (San Francisco: Jossey-Bass, 2013).

5. Alasdair C. MacIntyre, *After Virtue a Study in Moral Theory*, 3rd ed. (South Bend, IN: University of Notre Dame Press, 2007), 68.

6. Sam A. Hardy and Gustavo Carlo, "Identity as a Source of Moral Motivation," *Human Development* 48 (2005): 232–56.

7. Taylor, *The Sources of the Self*, 28.

8. Thomas Lickona, *Educating for Character: How Our Schools Can Teach Respect and Responsibility* (New York: Bantam, 1991).

9. William Damon, "Self-Understanding and Moral Development from Childhood to Adolescence," in *Morality, Moral Behavior, and Moral Development*, eds. William M. Kurtines and Jacob L. Gewirtz (New York: Wiley, 1984).

10. The inspiration for this distinction comes from Matthew Davidson, Thomas Lockona, and Vladimir Khmelkov, "Smart & Good Schools: A New Paradigm for High School Character Education," in *Handbook of Moral and Character Education*, eds. Larry P. Nucci and Darcia Narvaez (New York: Routledge, 2008), 370–90.

11. Willem Wardekker and Siebren Miedema, "Denominational School Identity and the Formation of Personal Identity," *Religious Education* 96, no. 1 (2001): 37.

12. See Wardekker and Miedema, "Denominational School Identity"; Taylor, *The Sources of the Self*; Alasdair MacIntyre, *After Virtue*; and Alasdair MacIntyre, *Three Rival Versions of Moral Enquiry: Encyclopedia, Genealogy, and Tradition* (Lanham, MD: Rowman & Littlefield, 1990).

13. See for example *Journal of Counseling & Development* 77 (Winter 1999): 4–53.

14. Christian Smith, *What is a Person?* (Chicago: University of Chicago Press, 2010), 50–51. This use of the term "identity" should not be confused with the term "moral identity" developed by Augusto Blasi in psychology (see chapter 2).

15. See John Witte Jr., *From Sacrament to Contract: Marriage, Religion, and Law in the Western Tradition*, rev. ed. (Louisville, KY: Westminster/John Knox Press, 2012).

16. Lawrence Kohlberg, *The Philosophy of Moral Development: Moral Stages and the Idea of Justice, Essays on Moral Development* (San Francisco: Harper and Row Publishers, 1981), 1–9.

17. Jason Baehr, "The Varieties of Character and Some Implications for Character Education," *Journal of Youth and Adolescence* 46 (2017): 1153–61.

18. Baehr, "The Varieties of Character."

19. K. Anders Ericsson and Robert Pool, *Peak: Secrets from the New Science of Expertise* (New York: Houghton Mifflin Harcourt Publishing Company, 2016), 14.

20. Albert Bandura, *Self-Efficacy: The Exercise of Control* (New York: Freeman, 1997).

21. Ericsson and Pool, *Peak*, 15.

22. For more examples see Ericsson and Pool, *Peak*.

23. Ronald Gallimore and Roland Tharp, "What a Coach Can Teach a Teacher, 1975–2004: Reflections and Reanlysis of John Wooden's Teaching Practices," *The Sports Psychologist* 19, no. 2 (2004): 119–37.

24. See Rafe Esquith, *Teach Like Your Hair's on Fire: The Methods and Madness Inside Room 56* (New York: Viking, 2007).

25. Ericsson and Pool, *Peak*, 60.

26. *Jump Shot: The Kenny Sailors Story*, accessed May 1, 2022, https://www.jumpshotmovie.com/.

27. Christopher Peterson and Martin E. P. Seligman, *Character Strengths and Virtues: A Handbook and Classification* (New York: American Psychological Association; Oxford University Press, 2004), 303–4.

28. John Mearsheimer, "The Aims of Education Address," *The University of Chicago Record* 32 (1997): 5–8 and David Brooks, "The Organizational Kid," *Atlantic Monthly*, April 2001, 53.

29. Harry R. Lewis, "The Freshman Pledge," *Bits and Pieces* (blog), August 30, 2011, http://harry-lewis.blogspot.com/2011/08/freshman-pledge.html.

30. Harvard College, "Mission, Vision, and History," accessed May 1, 2022, https://college.harvard.edu/about/mission-vision-history.

Chapter 2

The Most Important Ingredients for Moral Motivation

From the Sociological to the Philosophical, Psychological, and Moral Frames

Among our [moral] exemplars, we saw no "eking out" of moral acts through intricate, tortuous cognitive processing. Instead, we saw an unhesitating will to act, a disavowal of fear and doubt, and a simplicity of moral response. Risks were ignored and consequences went unweighed.

—Anne Colby and William Colby, *Some Do Care: Contemporary Lives of Moral Commitment*[1]

Many people today have heard about the ten thousand-hour rule. Unfortunately, the rule is usually a misunderstood application from the research of K. Anders Ericsson, mentioned in the previous chapter. Ericsson did not find that excellence comes by merely practicing ten thousand hours. The key, he found, is not the amount of the time spent practicing, but rather the particular type of practice (deliberate practice) under a wise coach.

Ericsson noted that although deliberate practice is vital to becoming an expert, it is not "inherently enjoyable."[2] As a result, he observed that deliberate practice does not nurture one's initial motivation. It may perhaps help one continue one's motivation in that often "individuals are motivated to engage in [practice] by its instrumental value in improving performance."[3]

Furthermore, he does muse regarding the deliberate practice needed to become excellent at some endeavor, "The practice itself may lead to physiological adaptations that produce more enjoyment and more motivation to do that particular activity. That is nothing but speculation at this point, but it

33

is reasonable speculation."[4] In other words, unlike the argument offered by certain recent ethicists and philosophers, Ericsson found *there is no current empirical evidence that you can simply practice yourself into initially loving something.*[5]

In fact, the call to engage in ten thousand hours of deliberate practice under demanding mentors can be a call to burn oneself out. After all, practice requiring self-control takes energy, and can lead to exhaustion or exasperation.[6] We all know of young athletes, musicians, and students led to burnout by overly pushy moms, dads, coaches, and mentors. Indeed, a child may find an initial reason to want to improve their performance and achieve identity excellence from wanting to please parents, coaches, or teachers, but that motivation rarely lasts (and it is considered unhealthy if it does).

In the realm of moral education, the psychologist Lawrence Kohlberg identified this problem in the moral domain where, he argued, the problem is not only pushy and controlling parents or teachers but also governments. He called it *socialization* of a hidden or overt set of virtues or values.[7] Others would simply term it indoctrination. Kohlberg noted that although the Soviet Union may be fine socializing a vision for moral education that does not respect the autonomy or individual rights of students, moral education in a liberal democracy should not only respect autonomy but teach respect for moral autonomy.[8]

Not surprisingly, we find the respect for some degree of autonomy is an important component in the development of expertise as well. Ericsson concluded regarding the importance of individual motivation, "Interested individuals need to be engaging in the activity and motivated to improve performance before they begin deliberate practice."[9] In other words, since practice is often unenjoyable, someone must be motivated to even *start* an endeavor. Moral goals especially need particular types of moral motivation. Unlike learning to be excellent in golf, moral goals are not simply self-derived. As Anne Colby and William Damon point out:

> Rather, moral goals are drawn from considerations extending well beyond any individual's personal inclinations and interests. These considerations may include concerns about another's welfare; about the welfare of society as a whole; about one's duties and responsibilities; about cultural rules and regulations; about matters of honor, honesty, and integrity; or about a number of other norms and principles. . . . There is always an obligatory element in moral goals, and they are always attached to social reality, spiritual sentiment, or religious tradition.[10]

This chapter addresses this question of what motivates the pursuit of identity excellence and what sustains its continuation.

REASONS FOR CROSSING THE MOTIVATIONAL RUBICON TO IDENTITY EXCELLENCE

One of the intriguing things about theories of motivation is how they often describe the process of choosing a goal in rather deliberate ways, but they do not exactly probe the mystery of what converts someone to a goal. For example, Heinz Heckhausen's Rubicon model explores *how* the motivational process toward goals progresses.[11] Typical of modern theories from the 1980s, the first deliberation phase takes a rational actor approach which sees subjects "weigh the desirability and feasibility of their many wishes."[12]

Similarly, another common motivational theory, expectancy-value theory, posits that someone chooses a goal because of its desirability/value and its feasibility/expectancy. Perhaps someone desires and sees it as feasible to become an excellent friend or excellent caretaker of the earth. But why do they choose this goal beyond simple situational or personal factors (e.g., personality traits)? Heckhausen has argued that one may be motivated by "superordinate identity goals," but all of us have many identities in which we may not initially value identity excellence but later we do.[13] What persuades someone's conversion to this switch?

When it comes to moral goals such as identity excellence, other scholars have recognized that people are similarly motivated by these kinds of realistic fantasy narratives.[14] The morally transformative power of such narratives has long been known throughout history. Whether it is Harriet Beecher Stowe's *Uncle Tom's Cabin*, and its influence on the abolition movement in the United States, or Nikolai Chernyskevsky's *What Is to Be Done?* and its influence on Vladimir Lenin and the Communist Party in Russia, certain narratives can inspire revolutionary moral transformation (for good or ill).

Scholars find individuals desire to be involved in *a particular identity community guided by a larger ideal identity narrative.* Such narratives situate one's particular activities within a larger current drama that also contains moral ideals. By immersing oneself in such a drama, one's activity acquires meaning and purpose—some kind of ultimate significance, emotive power, and behavioral significance.

When motivated by a moral/sacred narrative within a community that engages all the moral elements mentioned in the last chapter, something slowly happens to our identity. Interestingly, Ericsson writes about the change in identity that happens to young people on the road to identity excellence. He explains that the young students seeking excellence "saw themselves as 'pianists' or 'swimmers' by the age of eleven or twelve, or as 'mathematicians' before they turned sixteen or seventeen."[15]

In the process of becoming excellent within a community with an over-arching drama or narrative, they began to identify with the identity for which they were pursuing excellence. As a result, they underwent changes in their understanding of the self that resulted in the integration of one's self and per-formative ways of thinking to develop an identity. Although Ericson is not a moral educator, moral educators have also started to recognize the importance of this process: what they call the acquisition of moral identity.

This chapter examines the importance of moral identity development for acquiring moral excellence and moral expertise. It maintains that by the time a student reaches college, they have integrated many such identities in their sense of self and established what it means to be "good" versions of those identities. How higher education can help students develop sophisticated forms of moral identity in multiple areas of identity requiring expertise is one of the challenges it faces.

NATURE, SOCIAL IDENTITY, AND IDENTITY EXCELLENCE

With any quest for identity excellence, we are born into a drama already occurring. In rare instances, someone may invent their own drama and quest in a sliver of life, but for the vast majority of human beings and life, this drama and quest is already constructed. For example, in basketball, we inherit an already established setting in which we need a basket, a ball, a court, four teammates, and an opposing team of five players.

Moreover, the sociological field is set. There are already organized leagues at every level from professional leagues to leagues for young children. Of course, this does not mean new leagues cannot be created or new ways of playing cannot be devised (3-on-3 half court, lowering the goal, etc.), but we must recognize that anything created can only be created in relationship to what already was created in the history of an identity and its associated tradi-tion of identity excellence.

The same proves true with more general human practices such as marriage. We inherit various moral traditions of marriage related both to religious and philosophical moral traditions. What role do the state, religion, families, civil society (i.e., nongovernmental communities), or nature play? Furthermore, whereas in the past, religious institutions may have developed various moral and legal structures (e.g., canon law) to regulate marriage, today every coun-try regulates marriage. Those legal systems in our countries may or may not permit polygamy or same-sex marriage, and they may or may not prosecute people for adultery. Thus, we need to understand how prior natural and socio-logical systems shape our understanding of identity and identity excellence.

The relationship between social structures and the cultivation of identity excellence has long been identified by sociology. Charles Ellwood explained this point over a hundred years ago when the discipline was first emerging. In his article, "The Sociological Basis of Ethics," he wrote:

> Accordingly, each form of association, and especially each institution, has its appropriate virtues, and these virtues, as we have said, are not mere abstractions, but are concrete realities in the social life. Thus, the family for example, has its appropriate virtues. We cannot conceive such a virtue as chastity existing apart from such an institution as the family. While this virtue may have certain metaphysical implications, yet practically, chastity exists for the sake of the family and not merely as an abstract virtue in itself.[16]

The development of a particular virtue often only makes sense within a particular identity and its narrative and perceived purpose.

Furthermore, sociologists have observed that, through education, children are socialized into these social structures and particular visions of identity excellence that existed before them. In this regard, different groups in society already provide the different visions of identity excellence into which individuals are immersed. Children then internalize these moral visions initially with little critical thought.[17]

Most sociological or social psychology theories regarding identity (e.g., personal identity theory, role identity theory, social identity theory, identity control theory) recognize this point, although they perhaps point to different aspects of human agency involved in this process.[18] For example, Sheldon Stryker's identity theory tends to prioritize the role of social structures in forming one's identity expectations over individual agency.

Yet, the theory acknowledges that individuals both have multiple identities and order them according to salience. Stryker defines salience as "the likelihood that a given identity will be invoked or called into play in a variety of situations; alternatively, it can be defined as the differential likelihood across persons that a given identity will be invoked in a given situation."[19] The higher an identity within the salience hierarchy, the more likely it is that an individual will enact that role when social situations allow.

Certainly, there are both natural and sociological structures that determine some of these identities. For example, some identities, such as being a son or daughter, are almost always the result of a natural process, but they have thick moral traditions associated with what it means to be a good son or daughter. Marriage also emerges out of these natural processes as does the identity of grandparent, aunt, uncle, etc.

Yet, there are other identities that are much more pure social creations (e.g., social worker), and the standards of moral excellence associated with being a social worker are much more tied to the professional community created by that particular social organization. Identities in these cases, and in the cases of nonprofit advocacy groups or political organization identities (e.g., ACLU member, Libertarian), are better explained by collective identity theory, which emphasizes the human agency and activity involved in the creation of such social organizations and identities.

No matter how such identities are created, the question emerges: To what degree are moral expectations simply role expectations that one unconsciously internalizes (e.g., "I need to call my mother once a day/week") as opposed to consciously chosen personal performance expectations (e.g., "Unlike my own parents who did not attend my events or do anything with me, I will be there for my children at their events and take them places during my free time")?

For example, perhaps one seeks consciously to form one's cognition, affections, and behavior in line with a particular social group's vision of identity excellence (e.g., southerners show hospitality, Muslims care about submission and obedience to God).[20] Similar to sociology, psychology has also sought to understand the process of moving from external social expectations associated with an identity to making it part of one's own identity—what they call moral identity development.

THE DISCOVERY OF MORAL IDENTITY: THE PSYCHOLOGICAL FRAME

Although Lawrence Kohlberg identified the problem with simple socialization in the 1970s, he unfortunately took a very narrow approach to addressing it. He concluded that a moral expert is someone who reasons morally at a certain level and that the person who reasons this way has developed the virtue of justice. Thus, he maintained that for public schools in liberal democracies, "the only constitutionally legitimate form of moral education in the schools is the teaching of justice and the teaching justice in the schools requires just schools."[21]

Unfortunately, as James Davison Hunter notes in *The Death of Character*, Kohlberg's approach proved largely ineffective. In fact, Hunter goes so far as to claim "fundamental aspects of his 'just community' experiment in democratic education in the Cluster School' proved to be nothing less than a social and moral fiasco."[22]

In the 1980s, a group of developmental psychologists became concerned that Kohlberg's approach to ethics focused too much on the cognitive component of moral development. They noted that there was little evidence that greater moral understanding actually led to consistent moral action.[23] As part of their proposed corrective to Kohlberg's theory, they formulated approaches that considered what they called the moral self or moral identity. Three figures played a particularly important role in the development of this concept: William Damon, Anne Colby, and Augusto Blasi.

William Damon and Anne Colby

In the 1980s, Stanford psychologist William Damon discovered through his research on children and adolescents that younger children's concept of the self was separate from their conceptions of moral domain. However, as they matured into adolescence, these conceptual systems merged. This merging would continue throughout adulthood, sometimes only partially and, at other times, more completely. In other words, the individual moved from seeing morality as externally imposed to part of one's self.

This basic finding would be reinforced by Damon's research in collaboration with Carnegie Foundation scholar Anne Colby regarding moral exemplars. They found, "When there is perceived unity between self and morality, judgment and conduct are directly and predictably linked, and action choices are made with great certainty."[24] Although they did not initially use the term "moral identity," they would later adopt the term from Augusto Blasi who did the most to advance the concept.

Augusto Blasi

Like Damon and Colby, Blasi's concept of moral identity also grew out of dissatisfaction with the ability of Kohlberg's model to explain moral actions. Blasi found that having higher-level moral reasons for doing something (á la Kohlberg) did not necessarily mean that one would be motivated to moral action.[25] Instead, he recognized that the impetus for moral action often starts from a sense of one's identity. He used "moral identity" to refer to the *internal* human understanding and desires related to our interaction with externally existing and inherited conceptions of identity excellence.

Blasi, thereby, contended that a moral identity refers to the internalization, adoption, and use of these frameworks. It requires an understanding that a particular moral action is demanded or required by that identity, and the recognition that self-consistency requires engaging the action. In other words, when an individual takes on an identity, they do so with an understanding of the moral ideal toward which it orients.

We acquire this moral ideal through the combination of the cultural moral tradition associated with the identity as it has been taught to us, our revisions of certain parts of a tradition, the incorporation of other parts, or even newly imagined aspects. Overall, a desire for authenticity and integrity pushes us to pursue the moral ideal established through these means.

Blasi's view had its roots in the work of philosopher Harry G. Frankfurt and his distinction between persons and wantons. Frankfurt described a wanton as someone who simply has desires but does not care to reflect upon the desirability of those desires or how to order those desires. In contrast, a "person" is someone who has desires about desires, what he calls "second-order desires." Persons care about the motives and first-order desires one has in life and seeks to prioritize them according to a particular moral order derived from larger narratives or belief systems.[26]

Blasi made the distinction between the person without a moral identity (similar to the wanton) and the person with a moral identity. He says of the person lacking a moral identity:

> [They] will still understand and use moral speech, will be able to make moral judgments and to engage in discussions about the appropriateness of certain moral decisions and the validity of certain moral criteria [aka Kohlberg's dilemmas and stages]. However, a moral perspective will play no significant role in his or her life, in the decisions that really matter, in the fundamental outlook on the world and on history, or in eliciting strong emotions and deep anxieties.[27]

The person who lacks a moral identity has not incorporated moral concepts and desires, through habit or willful decision, into their reflexive or deliberate decision-making processes.

In contrast, a person who has an internal moral identity *uses* their second-order desires, which stem from their ideal moral order—developed in interaction with existing moral traditions—and applies them to their life. The result is that "certain spontaneous emotions and desires are integrated, appropriated, owned; others, whether or not one succeeds in controlling them, are disowned and rejected as not fitting with the emotions one wants to have or the person one wants to be."[28]

The person having a moral identity may draw upon a whole variety of external moral virtues, principles, and ends to inform their ideal moral order. While some feel that these virtues, principles, and ends are natural givens by God or the universe, others believe they are socially or individually chosen. In both cases, these elements of the moral order are chosen, internalized, and actively drawn upon when making decisions.

This process allows the person to reconcile objective identities (e.g., what it means to be an excellent friend, neighbor, or citizen) with their associated moral order. Bergman summarized this approach as it relates to moral motivation in this way,

> The objective, the morally rational, is not imposed but rather *chosen* by the subject in the subject's freedom of will. By such free choosing the subject

shapes his or her own identity, and thereby his or her own will itself, in light of objective moral reality but not in simple obedience, internalization, or socialization . . . moral understanding *acquires* motivational power *through its integration into the structures of the self*, into one's moral identity.[29]

In addition, there are two particular internalized virtues that help with this process: responsibility and integrity. The person with a moral identity has a sense that they should act a certain way to be morally consistent. Blasi summarized his view in this way:

1. Moral understanding more reliably gives rise to moral action if it is translated into a judgment of personal responsibility.
2. Moral responsibility is the result of integrating morality in one's identity or sense of self.
3. From moral identity derives a psychological need to make one's actions consistent with one's ideals.[30]

Thus, when a person has integrated morality into their sense of self, they will feel a responsibility to act in a way that is congruent with the moral order undergirding their sense of morality. For example, if a person identifies themself as trustworthy, they will feel a responsibility to avoid deceitful behavior because it would be inconsistent with their moral identity and sense of self.

It is also worth pointing out, in this example, that a person who identifies as trustworthy is not the only person capable of avoiding deceit. That said, the latter have not formed a moral identity based in trustworthiness and will, therefore, be less likely to feel a responsibility to consistency. In later research, Blasi provided substantial evidence of his view that only a certain percentage of people construct a moral identity.[31]

It is important to recognize the difference between Blasi's view and the overly cognitive approach to ethics represented by Kohlberg. Daniel Lapsley summarized the difference between Blasi and Kohlberg in this way, "For Kohlberg, moral motivation to act comes from one's fidelity to the prescriptive nature of moral principles. . . . Hence not to act is to betray a principle. For Blasi, in contrast, moral motivation to act is a consequence of one's moral identity, and not to act is to betray the self."[32] Blasi's view, often seen in the Christian tradition (e.g., Paul, Augustine), is that one of the most important identity wars occurs within oneself.[33] Sometimes, a person knows the good but does not do it. To Kohlberg, to know the good is to do the good. Blasi's account allows for the inner battle of being true to one's moral or ideal self and the respective goods that accord with that ideal—a tension we see in research related to honesty and deceit, such as cheating.

In addition, it is important to realize that for Blasi, and Damon and Colby for that matter, the moral understanding one has with a moral identity is not simply one's cognitive reasoning processes. As Colby explained, "Moral understanding includes not just conscious thought and rational judgment but implicit schemes or habits of interpretation that are internalized through participation in the cultures and social contexts in which development takes place. These aspects of moral understanding can influence moral identity along with conscious judgments about one's convictions."[34]

Colby astutely noted that we often are habituated to certain ways of thinking, feeling, and acting that do not involve conscious cognitive decision-making (although they perhaps once did). The argument in this book maintains we receive this inheritance for every identity we have. For instance, we inherit and internalize moral traditions about what it means to be a good friend, parent, neighbor, citizen, steward of the environment, and more.

The Influence of Blasi's Theory

Blasi's model has had significant influence in the field of moral psychology.[35] In the 1990s and early 2000s, some scholars began to explore further what might be involved with gaining a moral identity. One of the concepts that came to the fore was the idea of accessibility defined as "the activation potential of available knowledge."[36] According to this view, more frequently activated concepts from the inherited and internalized external moral tradition become more accessible and, in time, can be automatically accessed.[37] They can also be primed by others to encourage access, as was discussed regarding academic integrity.

When applied to the moral domain, Lapsley and Narvaez argued:

> [M]oral categories that are essential, central, and important to one's self-understanding would be ones that are chronically accessible for interpreting the social landscape. Such categories would be constantly "on-line," or at least easily activated and readily primed for processing social information. And once activated these moral constructs would dispose the individual to interpret and judge situations along moral lines.
>
> In addition, the social cognitive perspective would suggest that traits, virtues and other dispositional features of moral character are better conceptualized in terms of cognitive-affective units: personal constructs and knowledge structures, categories and schemes that are chronically accessible. Virtuous individuals by this account would be those for whom moral categories are chronically accessible for appraising and interpreting the social landscape.[38]

In other words, for the development of one's moral identity, it is less important that they reason at a certain cognitive stage and more important that they learn to access moral frameworks and concepts easily, have them constantly "on-line," and desire to use them.

How does one acquire these concepts and get them "on-line"? One line of research has found that moral identity is brought on-line by situational cues. As Lapsley and Hardy summarized the finding from research exploring this question, "Situational cues can activate or deactivate the accessibility of moral identity, or else activate some other identity at odds with morality. A situation that primes or activates the accessibility of moral identity strengthens the motivation to act morally. Situational factors that decrease accessibility weaken moral motivation."[39]

Recent studies have confirmed this reality. One group of scholars concludes, "We see moral identity as a core motivational element in the emerging sense of young adulthood."[40] Scholars have also produced an array of studies to support other pivotal aspects of moral identity theory. These studies find that people who have a well-developed sense of moral identity and draw upon it in their thinking and motivation demonstrate a host of positive qualities. They show greater moral regard for out-groups and include more people in their circle of moral responsibility.[41] They are more empathetic, principled, academically honest, and morally attentive.[42]

In addition, they show greater moral pleasure and elation in acts of goodness and are more willing to give time to prosocial causes.[43] Finally, exhibiting a highly developed moral identity predicts positive psychological well-being and health such as higher levels of self-esteem and lower levels of anxiety, risk behaviors, and depression.[44] Overall, a meta-analysis of 111 studies on the topic concluded that "moral identity was found to be significantly associated with moral behavior."[45]

Study participants also revealed less negative ethical behavior. They demonstrated less unethical behavior at work and less organizational deviance.[46] They were less likely to demean out-groups, morally disengage, rationalize harm to others, or engage in aggressive actions.[47] In light of this research, one wonders why the development of moral identity has not been a central focus of curricular and student affairs work in higher education.

So how does one develop a moral identity? The research in this area is in its infancy, although certain elements have emerged.[48] One does not simply self-author moral frameworks and bring them "on-line." Instead, one first learns these moral frameworks by being part of a community of practice that incarnates these frameworks. One longitudinal study of seventeen-to nineteen—year-olds found that involvement in community activities was correlated with a higher endorsement of virtues such as trustworthiness, honesty, fairness, justice, care, integrity, and benevolence.

Moreover, scholars discovered that the formation of moral identity preceded from community involvement. In other words, "Community involvement by adolescents leads to the development of some sort of sense of identity that is characterized by a greater prominence of moral, prosocial values."[49] Follow-up to this longitudinal study found that part of the moral identity is formed by taking elements from these moral communities to co-construct and make sense of one's personal narrative and moral identity.[50]

In other studies of emerging adults who were considered moral exemplars, scholars discovered that the exemplars told life narratives that were more often characterized by agency themes, ideological depth, contamination sequences, redemptive experiences, and awareness of others' suffering than were the narratives of matched controls.[51] Of course, one way to achieve greater agency and ideological depth is to provide students with moral frameworks by which to think about and co-construct their life narratives. Unfortunately, as part II will reveal, higher education does not appear to provide students with these frameworks.[52]

Yet, simply providing the frameworks is not enough. For instance, the findings about moral identity can help one make sense of why many types of overly cognitive diversity training, bystander interventions, and Title IX awareness training are often ineffective.[53] They are ineffective because they do not successfully integrate the moral framework or content offered into the moral identity of the individual, and they do not seek deeper and more substantial character development of students. In short, they aim to communicate content—often in a one-time format intended to increase a student's cognitive complexity—rather than to help students see these important issues as a significant part of their moral identity for which they are responsible. If these topics are not part of a student's moral identity, they will not be accessible.

In sum, moral educators must realize the importance of internalizing the elements of identity excellence. Daniel Lapsley and Patrick L. Hill summarized the consensus:

> It is now a widely shared view that persons and situations interact in complex ways; that the person-situation distinction is a false one; that situational specificity and behavioral consistency are not antagonistic positions; and that traits are not static, non-developmental and immutable essences, but are instead organizational constructs that operate dynamically in transaction with environments.[54]

Thus, teaching students the key ingredients to identity excellence for each individual identity is not enough. One must also help students understand their multiple identities, recognize the visions of moral excellence associated with each of them, choose among those visions and then develop a moral identity for each of them.[55] Finally, as the next chapter reveals, learning how to order various identities is paramount to resolving conflicts between them.

NOTES

1. Anne Colby and William Damon, *Some Do Care: Contemporary Lives of Moral Commitment* (New York: The Free Press, 1992), 70.

2. K. Anders Ericsson, Ralf Th. Krampe, and Clemens Tesch-Romer, "The Role of Deliberate Practice in the Acquisition of Expert Performance," *Psychological Review* 100, no. 3 (1993): 363–406.

3. K. Anders Ericsson and Robert Pool, *Peak: Secrets from the New Science of Expertise* (New York: Houghton Mifflin Harcourt Publishing Company, 2016), 368.

4. Ericsson and Pool, *Peak*, 192.

5. See for example James K. A. Smith, *Desiring the Kingdom* (Grand Rapids, MI: Baker Academic, 2009) and certain essays in Stanley Hauerwas and Samuel Wells, eds., *The Blackwell Companion to Christian Ethics* (Malden, MA: Blackwell, 2004).

6. Rishi Sriram, Perry L. Glanzer, and Cara Allen Cliburn, "What Contributes to Self-Control and Grit? The Key Factors in College Students," *Journal of College Student Development* 59, 3 (2018): 259–73.

7. Lawrence Kohlberg, *The Philosophy of Moral Development: Moral Stages and the Idea of Justice, Essays on Moral Development* (San Francisco: Harper and Row Publishers, 1981), 1–7.

8. Kohlberg, *The Philosophy of Moral Development*, 29–48.

9. Ericsson and Pool, *Peak*, 371.

10. Colby and Damon, *Some Do Care*, 84.

11. Jutta Heckhusen and Heinz Heckhausen, *Motivation and Action*, 3rd ed. (New York: Springer, 2018). See especially the questions and phases in chapter 12.

12. Heckhusen and Heckhausen, *Motivation and Action*, e-book, location 18680.

13. Heinz Heckhausen, "Achievement Motivation and Its Constructs: A Cognitive Model," *Motivation and Emotion* 1, no. 4 (1977): 283–329.

14. Alasdair MacIntyre, *After Virtue*, 3rd ed. (South Bend, IN: University of Notre Dame Press, 2007). See also fantasy realization theory and Gabriele Oettingen, Hyeon-ju Pak, and Karoline Schnetter, "Self-Regulation of Goal Setting: Turning Free Fantasies about the Future into Binding Goals," *Journal of Personality and Social Psychology* 80, no. 5 (2001): 736–53.

15. Ericsson and Pool, *Peak*, 192.

16. Charles A. Ellwood, "The Sociological Basis of Ethics," *International Journal of Ethics* 20, no. 3 (April 1910): 323.

17. Sheldon Stryker, "Identity Theory and Personality Theory: Mutual Relevance," *Journal of Personality* 75, no. 6 (2007): 1083–1102.

18. For a helpful overview see Angie Andriot and Timothy J. Owens, "Identity," *Oxford Bibliographies*, https://www.oxfordbibliographies.com/view/document/obo-9780199756384/obo-9780199756384-0025.xml#obo-9780199756384-0025-div1-0009.

19. Stryker, "Identity Theory and Personality Theory," 1092.

20. Henri Tajfel, ed. *Social Identity and Intergroup Relations* (New York: Cambridge University Press, 1982).

21. Kohlberg, *The Philosophy of Moral Development*, 37.

22. James Davison Hunter, *The Death of Character: Moral Education in an Age without Good or Evil* (New York: Basic Books, 2000), 152.

23. Augusto Blasi, "Moral Identity: Its Role in Moral Functioning," in *Morality, Moral Behavior, and Moral Development*, eds. William M. Kurtines and Jacob L. Gewirtz (New York: Wiley, 1984), 128–39; Colby and Damon, *Some Do Care*.

24. Anne Colby and William Damon, "The Uniting of Self and Morality in the Development of Extraordinary Moral Commitment," in *The Moral Self*, eds. Noam, Gil G. and Thomas E. Wren (Boston: MIT Press, 1993), 150 (italics in original).

25. Augusto Blasi, "Moral Identity: Its Role in Moral Functioning," in *The Moral Self*. See also Augusto Blasi, "Moral Cognition and Moral Action: A Theoretical Perspective," *Developmental Review* 3 (1983): 178–210.

26. Harry G. Frankfurt, "Freedom of the Will and the Concept of a Person," *Journal of Philosophy* 68 (1971): 5–20.

27. Blasi, "Moral Identity," 132.

28. Augusto Blasi, "Emotions and Moral Motivation," *Journal for the Theory of Social Behaviour* 29, no. 1 (1999): 11.

29. Roger Bergman, "Why Be Moral? A Conceptual Model from Developmental Psychology," *Human Development* 45 (March/April 2002): 121 (italics in original).

30. Augusto Blasi, "The Development of Identity: Some Implications for Moral Functioning," 1993, 99.

31. Blasi, "The Development of Identity," 99.

32. Daniel Lapsley, *Moral Psychology* (Boulder, CO: Westview, 1996), 86.

33. Daniel K. Lapsley, "Moral Self-Identity as the Aim of Education," in *Handbook of Moral and Character Education*, eds. Larry P. Nucci and Darcia Narvaez (New York: Routledge, 2008), 37.

34. Anne Colby, "Moral Understanding, Motivation, and Identity," *Human Development* 45 (March/April 2002): 132.

35. Daniel K. Lapsley, "Moral Self-Identity as the Aim of Education," in *Handbook of Moral and Character Education*, eds. Larry P. Nucci and Darcia Narvaez (New York: Routledge, 2008), 30–52.

36. Daniel K. Lapsley and Darcia Narvaez, "Moral Psychology at the Crossroads," in *Character Psychology and Character Education*, eds. Daniel K. Lapsley and F. Clark. Power (South Bend, IN: University of Notre Dame Press, 2005), 29.

37. See Karl Aquino, Americus Reed, II, S. Thau, and Dan Freeman, "A Grotesque and Dark Beauty: How Moral Identity and Mechanisms of Moral Disengagement Influence Cognitive and Emotional Reactions to War," *Journal of Experimental and Social Psychology* 43 (2007): 385–92; Karl Aquino and Americus Reed, II, "The Self-Importance of Moral Identity," *Journal of Personality and Social Psychology* 83 (2002): 1423–40.

38. Lapsley and Narvaez, "Moral Psychology at the Crossroads," 30.

39 Daniel Lapsley and Sam A. Hardy, "Identity Formation and Moral Development in Emerging Adulthood," in *Flourishing in Emerging Adulthood: Positive Development During the Third Decade of Life*, eds. L. Padilla-Walker and L. Nelson (New York: Oxford University Press, 2017).

40. Michael W. Pratt, Mary Louise Arnold, and Heather Lawford, "Growing toward Care: A Narrative Approach to Prosocial Moral Identity and Generativity of Personality in Emerging Adulthood" in *Personality, Identity and Character: Explorations in Moral Psychology*, eds. Darcia Narvaez and Daniel K. Lapsley (New York: Cambridge University Press. 2009), 312; see also Keith Leavitt, Lei Zhu, and Karl Aquino, "Good without Knowing It: Subtle Contextual Cues Can Activate Moral Identity and Reshape Moral Intuition," *Journal of Behavioral Ethics* 137 (2015): 785–800; Karl Aquino, Dan Freeman, Americus Reed, II, Will Felps, and Vivien K. G. Lim, "Testing a Social-Cognitive Model of Moral Behavior: The Interactive Influence of Situations and Moral Identity Centrality," *Journal of Personality and Social Psychology* 97, no. 1 (2009): 123–41.

41. Americus Reed, II, and Karl F. Aquino, "Moral Identity and the Expanding Circle of Moral Regard toward Out-Groups," *Journal of Personality and Social Psychology* 84 (2003): 1270–86; Americus Reed, II, Karl F. Aquino, and E. Levy, "Moral Identity and Judgments of Charitable Behaviors," *Journal of Marketing* 71 (2007):178–93.

42. James R. Detert, Linda K. Trevino, and Vicki L. Sweitzer, "Moral Disengagement in Ethical Decision Making: A Study pf Antecedents and Outcomes," *Journal of Applied Psychology* 93, no. 2 (2008): 74–391; Brent McFerran, Karl. F. Aquino, and Michelle Duffy, "How Personality and Moral Identity Relate to Individuals' Ethical Ideology," *Business Ethics Quarterly* 30, no. 1 (2010): 35–56; Scott J. Reynolds, "Moral Attentiveness: Who Pays Attention to the Moral Aspects of Life?" *Journal of Applied Psychology* 93, no. 5 (2008): 1027–41; Scott A. Wowra, "Moral Identities, Social Anxiety, and Academic Dishonesty among American College Students," *Ethics & Behavior* 17, no. 3 (2007): 303–21.

43. Karl F. Aquino, Brent McFerran, and Marjorie Laven, "Moral Identity and the Experience of Moral Elation in Response to Acts of Uncommon Goodness," *Journal of Personality and Social Psychology* 100, no. 4 (2011): 703–718; Americus Reed, II, Adam Kay, Stephanie Finnel, Karl Aquino, and Eric Levy, "I Don't Want the Money, I Just Want Your Time: How Moral Identity Overcomes the Aversion to Giving Time to Prosocial Causes," *Journal of Personality and Social Psychology* 110, no. 3 (2016): 435–57.

44. Sam A. Hardy, Stephen W. Francis, Byron L. Zamboanga, Su Yeong Kim, Spencer G. Anderson, and Larry F. Forthun, "The Roles of Identity Formation and Moral Identity in College Student Mental Health, Health Risk Behaviors, and Psychological Well-Being," *Journal of Clinical Psychology* 69, no. 4 (2013): 364–82.

45. Steven G. Hertz and Tobias Krettenauer, "Does Moral Identity Effectively Predict Moral Behavior?: A Meta-Analysis," *Review of General Psychology* 20, no. 2 (2016): 129.

46. Rebecca L. Greenbaum, Mary B. Mawritz, David M. Mayer, and Manuela Priesemuth, "To Act Out, To Withdraw, or To Constructively Resist? Employee Reactions to Supervisor Abuse of Customers and the Moderating Role of Employee Moral Identity," *Human Relations* 66, no. 7 (2013): 925–50; D. R. May, Y. K. Chang, and R. Shao, "Does Ethical Membership Matter? Moral Identification and Its Organizational Implications," *Journal of Applied Psychology,* 100, no. 3 (2015): 681–94.

47. Isaac H. Smith, Karl F. Aquino, Spassena Koleva, and Jesse Graham, "The Moral Ties That Bind . . . Even to Out-Groups: The Interactive Effect of Moral Identity and the Binding Moral Foundations," *Psychological Science, 25* (2014): 1556–62; James R. Detert, Linda K. Trevino, and Vicki L. Sweitzer, "Moral Disengagement in Ethical Decision Making: A Study of Antecedents and Outcomes," *Journal of Applied Psychology*, 93 (2008): 374–91; Karl F. Aquino, Americus Reed, II, Stefan Thau, and Dan Freeman, "A Grotesque and Dark Beauty: How Moral Identity and Mechanisms of Moral Disengagement Influence Cognitive and Emotional Reactions to War," *Journal of Experimental Social Psychology* 43, no. 3: 385–92; Alvaro Q. Barriga, Elizabeth M. Morrison, Albert K. Liau, and John C. Gibbs, "Moral Cognition: Explaining the Gender Difference in Antisocial Behavior," *Merrill-Palmer Quarterly* 47, no. 4 (2001): 532–62.

48. Tobias Krettenauer and Steven Hertz, "What Develops in Moral Identities? A Critical Review," *Human Development* 58, no. 3 (2015): 137–53.

49. Michael W. Pratt, Bruce Hunsberger, Mark S. Pancer, and Susan Alisat, "A Longitudinal Analysis of Personal Values Socialization: Correlates of a Moral Self-Ideal in Late Adolescence," *Social Development* 12, no. 4 (2003): 579.

50. Pratt et al., "Growing toward Care."

51. William L Dunlop, Lawrence J, Walker, and M. Kyle Matsuba. "The Distinctive Moral Personality of Care Exemplars," *The Journal of Positive Psychology* 7, no. 2 (2012): 131–43; M. Kyle Matsuba and Lawrence J. Walker. "Young Adult Moral Exemplars: The Making of Self through Stories," *Journal of Research on Adolescence* 15, no. 3 (2005): 275–97;

Lawrence J. Walker and Jeremy A. Frimer. "Moral Personality of Brave and Caring Exemplars," *Journal of Personality and Social Psychology* 93, no. 5 (2007): 845–60.

52. Christian Smith with Kari M. Hojara, Hilary A. Davidson, and Patricia Snell Herzog, *Lost in Transition: The Dark Side of Emerging Adulthood* (New York: Oxford University Press, 2011).

53. Katerina Bezrukova, Chester S. Spell, Jamie L. Perry, and Karen A. Jehn, "A Meta-Analytical Integration of Over 40 Years of Research on Diversity Training Evaluations," *Psychological Bulletin* 142, no. 11 (2016): 1227–74.

54. Daniel K. Lapsley and Patrick L. Hill, "The Development of the Moral Personality," in *Personality, Identity, and Character: Explorations in Moral*, eds. Darcia Narvaez and Daniel K. Lapsley (New York: Cambridge University Press, 2009), 190.

55. Robert A. Emmons has found that we can pursue up to fifteen different goals at the same time; "Abstract versus Concrete Goals: Personal Striving Level, Physical Illness, and Psychological Well-Being," *Journal of Personality and Social Psychology* 62, 292–300.

Chapter 3

The Challenge of Ordering Our Multiple Identities for Excellence

Combining the Philosophical, Psychological, and Sociological Frames with Theology

I would say probably for me being a college student, and still being a daughter at the same time has been challenging, because I've had my own life here for the past three and a half years. And I have a life that is apart from my parents and I feel like my parents are still in the transition of learning how to parent an adult. And so we've gone through a lot of ups and downs of how to navigate that. And for me, it's been difficult to feel like I'm doing what's best for myself even if it's not what they want for me, or how to tell my parents 'no' in a healthy way because I, I'm allowed to do that or not feel bad or guilty about making certain decisions, even if it's not what they would want.

—College senior

The most important ethical issues in our lives have little to do with runaway trollies or whether we are going to steal a life-saving drug. The most important ethical conflicts (both in perception and of actual importance) concern how we prioritize and/or merge our identities in light of how we understand what it means to be excellent in those identities.

Said another way, the moral journey toward identity excellence involves not only learning to love a vision for excellence in such a way that it becomes an internalized moral identity that influences one's behavior, but also learning how to engage in this activity in multiple identities. Moreover, one must learn how to order the pursuit of identity excellence when—in the course

49

of pursuing identity excellence—the moral obligations of pursuing identity excellence come into conflict.

Of course, we do not always agree upon who we are or how we should prioritize our various identities. In fact, we often disagree on what our fundamental identity even should be. Consequently, this chapter explores how to assist in the complex endeavor of pursuing identity excellence considering multiple—sometimes conflicting—identity obligations.

MULTIPLE IDENTITIES AND MULTIPLE FORMS OF IDENTITY EXCELLENCE

As already mentioned in the last chapter, this approach has a significant amount in common with various identity theories in philosophy, psychology, and sociology that recognize that the self consists of multiple identities.[1] To help students recognize these identities, it helps to engage them in the following exercise. Ask students to write down all their identities using the following guide:

First name
Last name
Gender identity
Racial identity
Ethnic identity
National identity
Geographic identity
Vocational identity
Marital/Romantic identity
Son/Daughter
Father/Mother/None
Other family identities (e.g., uncle/aunt)
Neighbor
Broad religious identity (e.g., Jewish)
Specific religious identity (e.g., Reformed)
Political identity (e.g., Democrat/Republican)
Other ideological identity (e.g., vegan)
Ability identity (e.g., basketball/trumpet player)
College identity
Club identity (e.g., fraternity/sorority)
Sports team identity
Steward of money
Steward of culture

Caretaker of nature
Steward of one's body
Human
Any other identity

Once students understand their various identities, it is possible to assess the level of sophistication in their understanding of identity excellence for each. Often, students will have a very sophisticated understanding of what it means to be an excellent friend or American, according to the categories set forth in the last chapter, but they may have a very limited understanding of what it means to be a good neighbor or a caretaker of nature. The holistic moral educator concerned with human flourishing will help expand that understanding for every identity.

The Multi-identity Challenge

Importantly, achieving excellence in one identity context (e.g., husband or wife) does not mean that element will easily translate into another identity context (e.g., neighbor). We may love well at church, the synagogue, or the mosque while gossiping uncontrollably at school or work. We may courageously love with school friends but be cowards when interacting with strangers. In other words, we must consider what psychologists have "discovered" and most people recognize. Our behavior does not exhibit what scholars call cross-situational stability—consistency when living out our different identities.[2]

This understanding of identity excellence helps us understand past problematic conceptualizations of virtue. For instance, in psychology, the study of virtue was abandoned in the mid-twentieth century after a set of well-known studies by Hugh Hartshorne and Mark May claimed there was no such thing as stable character traits in people.[3] This odd conclusion was based on three findings (as summarized by Kohlberg):

1. You can't divide the world into honest and dishonest people. Almost everyone cheats some of the time; cheating is distributed in bell-curve fashion around a level of moderate cheating.
2. If a person cheats in one situation it doesn't mean he or she will or won't in another. There is very little correlation between situational cheating tests. In other words, it is not a character trait of dishonesty that makes children cheat in a given situation. If it were, you could predict they would cheat in a second situation if they did in the first.

3. People's verbal moral values about honesty have nothing to do with how they act. People who cheat express as much or more moral disapproval of cheating as those who don't cheat.[4]

If Harthorne and May would have paid more attention to how virtue is developed in the context of specific identities, they would have understood why they found cheating to vary by context. Just as jumping in ice skating is different than in basketball, being honest in marriage is enacted differently than being honest in one's profession.

This does not mean that there is no such thing as character; rather, it means character must be developed in specific contexts. That is why, as mentioned in the last chapter, Jason Baehr distinguishes between intellectual, moral, civic, and performance virtues and suggests we may need even more virtue categories. Different identity contexts require the unique development of virtues such as honesty, self-control, patience, justice, etc.

Thus, it is not surprising that there are different bags of virtue for teaching identity and its related telos. Moreover, even those virtues that transcend different identities (e.g., love) will look different among friends, lovers, and citizens (as the four ancient Greek words for love reveal).[5] Of course, some moral traditions maintain a belief that humans are all oriented toward one major overall telos. Consequently, such moral traditions hold that all people share a core human function and ought to develop certain associated virtues (e.g., love, justice, etc.); but, even in such cases there is a need to recognize that acquiring a particular virtue in different identity contexts will still look different.

This point is true for virtues, but it is also true for each element of identity excellence mentioned in chapter 1 (e.g., purpose, rules, practices, mentors, etc.). In fact, one could classify most of the rules associated with well-known moral lists, such as the Ten Commandments, as rules specific to identity contexts. Keeping the Sabbath pertains to excellence in one's relationship to God and stewarding one's body. Not committing adultery is a rule related to being an excellent spouse, although—as with any rule—it provides only a baseline standard versus a compelling moral vision for being an excellent spouse.

According to the conception presented thus far, this identity variance should be no surprise. We always learn the elements of excellence in the context of a particular identity role, and it is not easy to transfer excellence between roles. One may be quite creative in one's profession but lack creativity when thinking about how to celebrate a spouse's birthday in a loving way. Consequently, a seemingly simple virtue like love can become quite complicated in practice. Thus, contemplating how to be excellent in each identity domain proves necessary.

IDENTITY EXCELLENCE CONFLICT

Due to our different identities, our visions for identity excellence come into conflict at times. The major moral conflicts individuals continually experience in life involve ordering one's identities. The extent to which this proves true requires moving beyond the kinds of challenges that most philosophical ethicists or moral psychologists like to discuss (the moral conflicts about a moving trolley, stealing life-saving drugs, having sex with a sibling—presented by the likes of Phillippa Foot, Lawrence Kohlberg, and Jonathan Haidt).

Some theorists have recognized more common scenarios. For example, Sheldon Stryker mentioned how his interest in personal identity theory stemmed from a desire to explain a core moral question. He was interested in knowing "why one person takes his or her children to the zoo on a free weekend afternoon, while another person chooses to spend that time on the golf course with friends."[6] Stated morally, why does one person seek to be a good parent (or perhaps an insecure person who derives worth from pleasing one's children) and another person chooses to be a good friend (or perhaps just a selfish hedonist).

According to Stryker's personal identity theory, each person organizes their identities into a hierarchy based on identity salience and psychological centrality. As mentioned earlier, he defined identity salience as "the likelihood that a given identity will be invoked or called into play in a variety of situations" and psychological centrality as "the perceived importance to the person of an identity she/he holds."[7] For instance, to help students determine salience and psychological centrality regarding their identities, it helps to present them with a moral conflict to invoke a choice (e.g., a conflict between being a good student and being a good friend).

Both salience and psychological centrality (i.e., moral identity) are determined by what Stryker simply calls commitment. Most people spend their lives in various specialized, often small, social networks, "networks composed of persons to whom they relate by virtue of occupancy of particular social positions and the playing out of associated roles."[8] When one is committed to a social network, one commits to the identity or roles that network requires. Of course, one likely makes a moral commitment to be excellent in that identity or role. As Stryker summarizes, this commitment has moral implications, "To the degree that one's relationships to specific others depend[s] on being a particular kind of person, one is committed to being that kind of person."[9]

The commitment is both affective (related to the "depth of emotional attachment to particular sets of others in networks of relationship") and interactional. Stryker gives an example of the interactional commitment: "One can relate as husband not only to one's spouse, her friends, and her relatives but also to members of a couple's bridge club, 'gourmet' group, and other such groups."[10] One determines commitment, says Stryker, by determining "the costs of giving up meaningful relationships with others should persons pursue an alternative course of action in situations in which they are expected to play out a role in a given network."[11] To extend Stryker's illustration, the husband could decide to abandon both his emotional attachment to his wife and his interactional commitment, which would involve leaving or changing social network relationships.

Professors outside sociology have also recognized this identity conflict. Paul Bloom, a psychologist from Yale University, argues, "An evolving approach to the science of pleasure suggests that each of us contains multiple selves—all with different desires, and all fighting for control."[12] There's little surprise about this finding given the approach to understanding moral identity conflict just outlined. People face this issue every day. Should one be a good professional and work more on an upcoming class lecture or, instead, be a good spouse and/or parent and spend time with one's spouse and/or children? Individuals are constantly faced with the problem of determining how to integrate all these competing selves, desires, and loves into a cohesive understanding of their human personhood.

PROBLEMATIC APPROACHES TO CONFLICT BETWEEN VISIONS OF IDENTITY EXCELLENCE

Code-Switching

One solution to this problem involves a practice called code-switching. Jennifer Morton defines code-switching as "changing how one behaves as one moves between the community one is attempting to join and the one in which one's family and friends reside—in order to avoid incurring ethical costs and retain a sense of one's identity."[13]

As Morton notes later in her book, *Moving Up without Losing Your Way: The Ethical Costs of Upward Mobility*, people are always code-switching, particularly when seeking excellence in different identities. Visions of moral excellence with spouses, children, colleagues, parents, pets, neighbors, etc. often conflict.

Of course, for students who often navigate different cultural contexts during their lives—coming from Peru and going to Princeton to use Morton's example—code-switching can take place within just one identity. For instance, Morton talks about how she had to adjust to expectations about what it means to be an excellent woman as both a student at Princeton and as part of her family community in Peru. At Princeton, she found being assertive and individualistic was rewarded and that gender expectations were not as bifurcated. Yet when she returned home to Peru, she had to navigate a different reality:

> My gender was omnipresent. That category mapped onto different expectations back home. I had to tone down shows of ambition and assertiveness. I had to ignore the near-constant cat-calls on the street. When distant cousins came to visit, they all wanted to know what I ate and who I dated, but not what my thesis was about. My grandmother asked me whether I was making Peruvian food for my roommates. She looked disappointed when I rarely did. People commented on my weight. Living in America, they observed, makes everyone fatter. They didn't think commenting on my weight was out of bounds.[14]

Morton had to learn to code-switch on order to navigate ethical norms of gender excellence across multiple contexts. As she points out, these different ethical expectations create difficult ethical conflicts. Of course, everyone experiences such conflicts, whether within singular or across multiple identities.

So, how might one navigate competing moral traditions of identity excellence across multiple identities? After all, how someone prioritizes these aspects of their identity makes a key difference in how they think about the extent of their moral obligations. The same can be said of how one prioritizes a general understanding of human identity.

Choose Your Identity Tribe versus Find a Metaidentity that Enhances All Tribes

One way to solve the identity conflict problem is to socialize a group to choose particular identities as more important than others. In other words, one chooses one's identity tribe (e.g., American, White, female, upper class, Democrat, professionals). Unfortunately, this kind of arbitrary socialization has the tendency to ostracize and dehumanize those outside the tribe.

As such, a less problematic solution involves finding a common understanding of human identity that can both serve as a metaidentity and enhance the humanity of all. Discovering and establishing a primary identity means inheriting a vision for goodness that can encompass all other identities and, perhaps, all humanity. MacIntyre argues that in both the Greek and medieval Christian moral traditions, humans are understood as having "an essential nature and an essential purpose or function" so that "human" links to "good human" similar to the way in which "farmer" links to "good farmer."[15]

This approach has been undertaken most effectually in the Christian West. For instance, Avner Greif and Guido Tabellini maintain that one reason for the rise of the rule of law in the West pertains to the different identities used to establish moral obligation in the East and West.[16] If one's loyalty group—and thus one's scope of moral obligation—rests with one's clan, as it did in Confucian China, then a broad rule of law outside the clan—as well as organization building beyond the clan—becomes much more difficult.

In contrast to the East, Western Christians established a more generalized morality not based on clan identity, but rather on the claim that all humans are made in the image of God. These differences then applied to the moral obligations such as honor, contract, keeping, charity, and more. The identity one uses to determine one's moral obligations and understanding of virtue make a tremendous difference in the scope of one's moral obligations and how one views others with different subidentities.

Understanding everyone as made in God's image is unique in that the view holds that God enriches the dignity of all other creation-based identities instead of reducing them. In fact, the enriching and dignity-providing power of this reality has been demonstrated throughout history with philanthropy, health care, antislavery arguments, the expansion of universal education for women and the poor, and the abolition of slavery.

Gary Ferngren provides a helpful summary of some of the important developments that resulted from the emphasis on humans made *imago Dei* in the first four centuries of the church. One of the first areas where the understanding of the *imago Dei* in light of the incarnation contrasted sharply with previous pagan ethics. The central Christian virtue of *agape* was something one does because everyone is made in God's image. Moreover, as God loved humans through Christ, humans (image bearers of God) were also to love everyone in the same way (John 13:34–35).

One finds this expansion in early Christian writings as *The Clementine Homilies*, (circa 380 AD), "It behooves you to give honor to the image of God, which is man—in this wise: food to the hungry, drink to the thirsty, clothing to the naked, care to the sick, shelter to the stranger, and visiting him who is in prison, to help him as you can."[17] In line with Greif and Tabellini's earlier point, one extended agape not merely to your friends or tribe but to all humanity. In fact, Christians slowly helped change the ancient concept of *philanthropia* to be used as a synonym for agape in the early church by the fourth century.[18]

A second important change related to the overall view that among non-Christians, every human has worth or dignity. Ferngren observed that this belief was uncommon:

There was . . . little sympathy in early Greek literature for the physically impaired or oppressed, an attitude that can be demonstrated to have characterized both popular and official opinion in virtually every period of classical antiquity. Attitudes to the physically defective reflected the belief that health and physical wholeness were essential to human dignity, so much so that life without them was not thought to be worth living. Citizenship, kinship, status, merit, and virtue formed the foundation of claims to the possession of human rights or human worth. Those who lacked them (e.g., orphans, slaves, foundlings, the physically defective, prisoners) had no claim to the rights that they alone guaranteed or even to a recognition of their human worth.[19]

In contrast, the view that humans were made in God's image (and that God became human in Christ) magnified the intrinsic worth of all humans. This doctrine gave impetus for the preservation of all life including the poor, orphans, widows, the sick, and disabled. It also led to the repudiation of abortion, infanticide, and suicide.

Third, it also elevated the importance of the body. For the pagan acetic, the body was to be viewed negatively, but for Christians, bodily asceticism helped one war against spiritual forces of evil. Indeed, for Christians generally, "The Christian conception of Jesus as a perfect man contributed to raising the body to a status that it had never enjoyed in paganism."[20]

Fourth, viewing everyone as made in God's image redefined the poor. Christ had united God with the poverty-stricken human race. How much ore then should Christians seek to unite each other in solidarity as members of one body of Christ?

The influence of the imago Dei would later extend beyond these four things to the areas of slavery, education, and abolitionism. Thus, the imago Dei's fifth contribution is that it stirred the ideological arguments against slavery. For example, in an article about the roots of human dignity in late antiquity, Kyle Harper observed, "Few societies have been so squarely constructed on the institution of slavery as were ancient Greece and Rome."[21] As is well-known, Aristotle claimed in the *Politics*, "It is clear that there are certain people who are free and certain people who are slaves [by nature], and it is both to their advantage, and just, for them to be slaves," a claim that David Brion Davis noted "would help shape virtually all subsequent proslavery thought."[22]

In fact, we know of no pronouncements against slavery until an ancient Christian bishop, Gregory of Nyssa, made this astounding argument against slavery,

If a man makes that which truly belongs to God into his own private property, by allotting himself sovereignty over his own race, and thinks himself the master of men and women, what could follow but an arrogance exceeding all nature from

the one who sees himself as something other than the ones who are ruled? . . .
How much does rationality cost? How many obols for the image of God? How
many staters did you get for selling the God-formed man?[23]

He would go on to say that everything about humanity "manifests royal dignity" due to its "exact likeness to the beauty of the archetype."[24] As Harper
observes, "Gregory's vision of humanity was deeply stamped by his interpretation of *Genesis* and a profound reflection on the significance of humanity
as a creation in the image of God."[25]

Sixth, the theological doctrine of the imago Dei also had educational
implications in that it inspired the early architects of the medieval university. In the early medieval cathedral schools around Paris, and then in the
early University of Paris, thinkers were starting to work out the universal
educational implications of what it means to be made in God's image.[26] For
instance, Hugh of Saint Victor (1096–1141), an architect of one of the early
Parisian cathedral schools, maintained that we are all made in God's image,
but the fall marred this image. Thus, he claimed regarding education's purpose, "This is our entire task—the restoration of our nature and the removal
of our deficiency."[27]

This restoration involved receiving salvation from sin through Christ,
but it also involved a sanctification process that was both moral and educational. Hugh wrote about the need for *all* humans to discover and construct
a place for Wisdom in their heart and minds that adhered to a blueprint provided by God:

> Let no man excuse himself. Let no man say, "I am not able to build a house for
> the Lord; my poverty does suffice for such an expensive project; I have no place
> in which to build it." . . . You shall build a house for the Lord out of your own
> self. He himself will be the builder; your heart will be the place; your thoughts
> will supply the material.[28]

For Hugh, a Christian educational institution should assist with this majestic
endeavor by being God's instrument for helping rebuild the image of God
in humanity.

Unfortunately, the extent to which universities taught that *all* humans could
engage in this universal educational and sanctifying development of Wisdom
never took hold until four hundred years later. Why was this idea not advocated earlier within Christian universities for the earlier four centuries? Well,
for one, the incorporation of Aristotelian metaphysics and moral philosophy
into the liberal arts curriculum and mindset of society certainly did not help.
Aristotle's hierarchical understanding of human society that accepted slavery

and other social and educational inequities as natural, replaced and corrupted the more egalitarian Jewish and Christian view.

In fact, his writing about human identity and ethics elevated the role of reason for obtaining virtue (without the need of God's grace), promoted distinct social roles, and justified human inequality, Aristotle's *Nicomachean Ethics* and *Politics* became the primary course texts used in the moral philosophy classes of Christian medieval European universities for the next 350 years.[29] Universities taught the Aristotelian part in the "undergraduate" course on moral philosophy, and they taught Christian theology and ethics in the more advanced theology faculty.[30] Thus, "undergraduate" students educated only in the liberal arts would not build their understanding of humanity's core moral function on the concept of the imago Dei but on Aristotle's elitist and hierarchical understanding of humanity.

It was not until a radical higher education and curriculum reformer Pierre de la Ramée—commonly known as Peter Ramus—challenged the use of Aristotle and the teaching of pagan moral philosophy three hundred years later, which opened the way for revolutionary educational approaches grounded in Christian anthropology to once again bubble to the surface. During the decade prior to his death, Ramus criticized the extensive use of Aristotle in the teaching of ethics

> where the boy learns a mass of impieties: for example, that the principle and ideals of "the good" are innate in every man, that all the virtues are within his own power, that he acquires them by means of nature, art, and labor, and that for this work, so grand and so sublime, man has need of neither the aid nor the cooperation of God. Nothing about providence; not a word about divine justice; in short, since, in the eyes of Aristotle, souls are mortal, the happiness of man is reduced to this perishable life. Such is the philosophy out of which we build the foundation of our religion![31]

Instead of Aristotelian ethics, he wanted to make Christian theology foundational to the liberal arts in both metaphysics and moral philosophy.

Although his radical vision for changing metaphysics and moral philosophy had only limited influence in Reformed colleges and universities in France and the Netherlands, it was carried forward by a few significant Reformed radicals, one of them being the Ramsian Johann Heinrich Alsted.[32] Alsted would go on to educate Reformed Moravian thinker John Amos Comenius (1592–1670), the first major proponent of universal education for all people, including women and the poor.

Given Ramus's and Alsted's rejection of Aristotle's understanding of human identity, it is no surprise that Comenius focused on a Christian and not an Aristotelian understanding of human identity as well. The basis of his argument rested upon a specific Ramus-type rejection of Aristotle's social and hierarchical understanding of human identity. Comenius argued using the theological anthropology of the Hebrew scriptures:

> The following reasons will establish that not the children of the rich or the powerful only, but of all alike, boys and girls, both noble and ignoble, rich and poor, in all cities and towns, villages and hamlets, should be sent to school. In the first place, all who have been born . . . have been born with the same end in view, namely that they be . . . rational creatures, the lords of other creatures, and the images of their Creator. . . . God Himself has frequently asserted that with Him there is no respect of persons . . . so that, if, while we admit some to the culture of the intellect, we exclude others, we commit an injury not only against those who share the same nature as ourselves, but against God Himself.[33]

For Comenius, the idea that every human has dignity, a result of being made in God's image, has profound educational implications, namely, that educators should seek

> for the full power of development into full humanity not of one particular person or a few or even many, but of every single individual, young and old, rich and poor, noble and ignoble, men and women—in a word, of every human born on earth, with the ultimate aim of providing education to the entire human race regardless of age, class, sex and nationality.[34]

In other words, everyone made in the image of God, meaning all humans, need education for development.

Understanding that all humans are made in God's image led Comenius to the conclusion that there was no reason why women should be kept from education. He reasoned this way:

> They also are formed in the image of God and share in His grace and in the kingdom of the world to come. They are endowed with equal sharpness of mind and capacity for knowledge (often with more than the opposite sex), and they are able to attain the highest positions, since they have been called by God Himself to rule over nations, to give sound advice to kings and princes, to the study of medicine and of other things which benefit the human race. . . . Why, therefore should we admit them to the alphabet, and afterwards drive them away from books?[35]

Comenius' argument changed the dominant vision of who should be educated, regardless of the culture or context in which they lived.

Finally, the dignity inherent in divine image bearing also changed the vital political foundations of human society. Brad Gregory argues:

The modern secular discourse on human rights depends on retaining in some fashion—but without acknowledging—the belief that every human being is created in the image and likeness of God, a notion that could be rooted in nature so long as nature was regarded as creation whether overtly recognized as such or not.[36]

A state does not provide one with dignity and rights. It only protects what humans already have. As Thomas Jefferson noted, we are endowed with dignity and rights by our Creator.

Of course, Jefferson did not adequately articulate and enact the implications of this view for slavery. Unfortunately, it would take even longer for the key idea that we are *all* persons made in God's image to replace Aristotelian-type ideas used to justify human slavery. When one compares the arguments of the Christian abolitionists to the Christian defenders of slavery, one finds that the former constantly focused on a Christian doctrine that all humans are made in God's image while the defenders ignored it.

Thus, it should be no surprise to find that David Brion Davis's work, *Image of God: Religion, Moral Values, and Our Heritage of Slavery*, observes, "The popular hostility to slavery that emerged almost simultaneously in England and in parts of the United States drew upon the tradition of natural law and a revivified sense of the image of God in man."[37]

Thus, the southern abolitionist Angela Grimke argued, humanity "who was created in the image of his Maker, *never* can properly be termed a *thing*, though the laws of Slave States do call him 'a chattel personal.'"[38] Or, as the famous abolitionist Frederick Douglas proclaimed to a crowd in his famous Fourth of July speech, "You profess to believe 'that, of one blood, God made all nations of men to dwell on the face of all the earth,' [Acts 17:26] and hath commanded all men, everywhere to love one another; yet you notoriously hate, (and glory in your hatred), all men whose skins are not colored like your own."[39]

As can be seen by this cursory view, the idea that humans are made in God's image, as opposed to a focus on one's tribe, extended and enhanced humanity in numerous ways. Instead of alienating the poor, women, the handicapped, or those enslaved due to their race, it exalted them and helped enhance their humanity, bringing them new opportunities for identity excellence.

The Historical Answer from American Higher Education

This focus on the imago Dei also changed in early American moral education. As recounted in an earlier volume addressing the history of American moral education, the first moral philosophy text published in America did not even refer to the dominant Aristotelian ethics of the time.[40] The text, published by Thomas Clap—the first president of Yale—argued, "As Man was at first made in the moral Image or Likeness to God, so the recovery of that Image is the greatest duty and highest perfection."[41]

His rationale for why one should be like God was three-fold. Two of the reasons are ones often understood as animating Puritan ethics: 1) the law arises from God's will and 2) God, the creator, has sovereign power and authority his creation, humanity included. Yet how do we know that God's declaration is good? The answer, for Clap, arose from the third and most important reason for being like God: Our idea of good virtue comes "from the *infinite and absolute Perfection* of the divine Nature. For as God is the most perfect Being, so the most *perfect* state of any other Being, must consist in being *like to him.*"[42] Thus, if one wants to understand God, one needs revelation from God about God's character. Furthermore, if one wants to morally develop, one will want to develop God's virtues.

Clap's textbook was the first moral philosophy textbook in America, but it was also the last one to rely on a Judeo-Christian teleological foundation for identity. Not one moral philosophy textbook after Clap started by identifying humans as being made in God's image. His appeal that humans are made in God's image, and therefore God's likeness, as the foundational telos by which to understand what virtues to acquire (and to what degree), are not found in the works of any latter American moral philosophers.

MacIntyre noted, "It is when and only when the classical tradition in its integrity has been substantially rejected that moral arguments change their character so that they fall within the scope of some version of the "No 'ought' conclusion from 'is' premises" principle."[43] Understood in this way, the notion that we have a metaidentity as image bearers of God proves to be one of the most important keys to ethics. MacIntyre maintained that this loss of a functional human identity occurred during the Enlightenment, a conclusion supported by evidence from American moral education.[44] This situation has led to some problematic results, outlined in part II.

NOTES

1. For example see Sheldon Stryker, "Identity Theory and Personality Theory: Mutual Relevance: Contextualized Identities: Integrating Self-in-Context to Traditional Issues in Personality Psychology," *Journal of Personality* 75, no. 6 (2007): 1083–1102.

2. Kwame Appiah, *Experiments in Ethics* (Cambridge, MA: Harvard University Press, 2008).

3. Hugh Hartshorne Mark A. May, Julius Bernard Maller, and Frank K. Shuttleworth. *Studies in the Nature of Character, vol. 1; Studies in Deceit, vol. 2; Studies*

in Self-Control, vol. 3; *Studies in the Organization of Character, vol. 4* (New York: Macmillan, 1928–1930).

4. Lawrence Kohlberg, *The Philosophy of Moral Development: Moral Stages and the Idea of Justice, Essays on Moral Development* (San Francisco: Harper and Row Publishers, 1981), 34–35.

5. C. S. Lewis, *The Four Loves* (New York: Harcourt, Brace, 1960).

6. Stryker, "Identity Theory and Personality Theory," 1088.

7. Stryker, "Identity Theory and Personality Theory," 1092.

8. Stryker, "Identity Theory and Personality Theory," 1093.

9. Stryker, "Identity Theory and Personality Theory," 1093.

10. Stryker, "Identity Theory and Personality Theory," 1093.

11. Stryker, "Identity Theory and Personality Theory," 1093.

12. Paul Bloom, "First Person Plural," *The Atlantic*, November 2008, 90.

13. Jennifer M. Morton, *Moving Up without Losing Your Way: The Ethical Costs of Upward Mobility* (Princeton, NJ: Princeton University Press, 2019), 13.

14. Morton, *Moving Up without Losing Your Way*, 74.

15. Alasdair C. MacIntyre, *After Virtue a Study in Moral Theory*, 3rd ed. (South Bend, IN: University of Notre Dame Press, 2007).

16. Avner Greif and Guido Tabellini, "The Clan and the Corporation: Sustaining Cooperation in China and Europe," *Journal of Comparative Economics* 45, no. 1 (2017): 1–35.

17. As quoted in Gary B. Ferngren, *Medicine and Health Care in Early Christianity* (Baltimore, MD: Johns Hopkins University Press, 2009), 99.

18. Richard Finn, OP, *Almsgiving in the Later Roman Empire: Christian Promotion and Practice* (New York: Oxford University Press, 2006), 313–450.

19. Ferngren, *Medicine and Health Care in Early Christianity*, 95–96.

20. Ferngren, *Medicine and Health Care in Early Christianity*, 102.

21. Kyle Harper, "Christianity and the Roots of Human Dignity in Late Antiquity," in *Christianity and Freedom: Historical Perspectives*, eds. Timothy Samuel Shah and Allen D. Hertzke (New York: Cambridge University Press, 2016), 1–131.

22. David Brion Davis, *In the Image of God: Religion, Moral Values, and Our Heritage of Slavery* (New Haven, CT: Yale University Press, 2001), 128.

23. Gregory of Nyssa, *In Ecclesiasten*, 4.1. In *Sources chrétiennes* no. 416; Garnsey, *Ideas of Slavery*, 81–82.

24. Quoted in Andrew Louth, ed., *Ancient Christian Commentary on Scripture*, Genesis: 1–11, vol. 1 (Downers Grove, IL: IVP Academic, 2001), 34.

25. Harper, "Christianity and the Roots of Human Dignity in Late Antiquity," 133.

26. Walter Rüegg, "Themes," in *A History of the University in Europe: Vol. I. Universities in the Middle Ages*, ed. Hilde de Ridder-Symoens (Cambridge: Cambridge University Press, 1992), 32–33.

27. Hugh of St. Victor, *The Didascalicon of Hugh of St. Victor: A Medieval Guide to the Arts*, trans. Jerome Taylor (New York: Columbia University Press, 1991), 52.

28. Hugh of St. Victor, *De arca Noe morali* iv.i (PL, CLXXVI, 663B), quoted in Taylor, introduction, 171, note 132.

29. Laurence Brockliss, "Curricula," in *A History of the University in Europe: Vol. II; Universities in Early Modern Europe, 1500–1800*, ed. Hilde De Ridder-Symoens (Cambridge: Cambridge University Press, 1996), 578–89.

30. Gordon Leff, "The *Trivium* and the Three Philosophies," in *A History of the University in Europe: Vol. I. Universities in the Middle Ages*, ed. Walter Rüegg (Cambridge: Cambridge University Press), 307–36.

31. Peter Ramus, *Petri Rami Pro philosophica parisiensis academiae disciplina* (Paris, 1557), https://books.google.com/books?id=rFFV082xNp0C&pg=PA2&source=gbs_toc_r&cad=3#v=onepage&q&f=false. English translation is taken from Frank Pierrepont Graves, *Peter Ramus and the Educational Reformation of the Sixteenth Century* (New York: The MacMillan Company, 1912), 174–75.

32. Louthan and Sterk, "Introduction" in Jon Amos Comenius, *The Labyrinth of the World and the Paradise of the Heart*, trans. Howard Louthan and Andrea Sterk (New York: Paulist Press, 1998), 10.

33. Jon Amos Comenius, *The Great Didactic*, trans. M. W. Keatinge (London: Adam and Charles Black, 1907), 66.

34. Jon Amos Comenius, *Comenius's Pampaedia or Universal Education*, trans. A.M.O. Dobbie (Dover: Buckland Publications, 1986), 19.

35. Comenius, *The Great Didactic*, 68.

36. Brad Gregory, *The Unintended Reformation: How a Religious Revolution Secularized Society* (Cambridge, MA: Harvard University Press, 2012), 381.

37. David Brion Davis, *Image of God: Religion, Moral Values and Our Heritage of Slavery* (New Haven, CT: Yale University Press, 2001), 198. See also Dierdre N. McCloskey, *Bourgeois Equality: How Ideas, Not Capital or Institutions, Enriched the World* (Chicago: University of Chicago Press, 2016).

38. Angelina Emily Grimké, *Appeal to the Christian Women of the South* (New York: American Anti-Slavery Society, 1836), accessed September 12, 2021, http://utc.iath.virginia.edu/abolitn/abesaegat.html, 3.

39. Oration, Delivered in Corinthian Hall, Rochester by Frederick Douglass, July 5, 1852 (Rochester: Lee, Mann & Co., 1852), accessed September 12, 2021, 36.

40. Thomas Clap, *An Essay on the Nature and Foundation of Moral Virtue and Obligation: Being a Short Introduction to the Study of Ethics: For the Use of the Students of Yale-College* (New Haven, CT: B. Mecom, 1765), 53 (italics in the original). See Perry L. Glanzer, *The Dismantling of Moral Education: How Higher Education Reduced the Human Identity* (Lanham, MD: Rowman & Littlefield, 2022).

41. Clap, *An Essay on the Nature and Foundation of Moral Virtue*, 54.

42. Clap, *An Essay on the Nature and Foundation of Moral Virtue*, 8–9 (italics in original).

43. MacIntyre, *After Virtue*, 69.

44. Glanzer, *The Dismantling of Moral Education.*

PART II

The Problems with Contemporary Collegiate Moral Education

Using the Frames for Critical Analysis

There is no convincing defensible strategy behind the undergraduate curriculum, and the more intelligent students and the more self-critical faculty know this.

—Sir Eric Ashby, 1971[1]

Using the understanding of moral excellence and identity developed in part I, we can now understand some of the problems with how higher education currently approaches moral education. Early in the history of higher education in America, one finds that American moral philosophers and educators gave up relying upon a functional view of a person's humanity, what I call a metaidentity, connected to Jewish-Christian metaphysics (i.e., we are all made in God's image).[2]

Despite this choice, they did not give up a teleological understanding of ethics. Without a thick understanding of human flourishing and the human telos, American colleges and universities simply appealed to narrower slices of identity that resulted in narrower forms of focus and moral reasoning (e.g., be a gentleman, be a person of honor, be a good professional). In addition, they often turned less to moral reasoning as a means of persuading students and more to various forms of identity socialization. Yet turning to mere fragments of identity to guide moral education promotes diminished forms of socialization and narrow forms of moral reasoning.

Universities today draw upon a limited range of common identities with certain kinds of purposes, rules, virtues, practices, and wisdom, but they ignore whole swathes of human identity and the moral life. As a result, large areas of the university, including general education, professional education, and cocurricular life, stand in moral chaos. The chapters in this part help us understand that chaos.

NOTES

1. Sir Eric Ashby as quoted by John H. Knowles, "Clarity of Thought and Higher Education," *Our Third Century: Directions, Committee on Government Operations, United States Senate* (Washington, DC: U.S. Government Printing Office, 1976), 181.

2. For a historical examination of this problem see Perry L. Glanzer, *The Dismantling of Moral Education: How Higher Education Reduced the Human Identity* (Lanham, MD: Rowman & Littlefield, 2022).

Chapter 4

The Ethically Challenged Curriculum

General Education

More generally, students have come to expect high grades for little work in Gen Ed courses; this is a source of dissatisfaction from students and faculty alike.

—Harvard General Education Review Committee Interim Report, 2015[1]

Most undergraduates think general education is a waste of time. One can peruse previous scholarship or the internet for opinion polls, faculty evaluations, and student opinions, but the conclusions of a recent report from Harvard's faculty committee evaluating their new general education program provides an example of what any professor at any institution will know:

- Students report not taking their Gen Ed courses as seriously as other courses.
- Students wish more Gen Ed courses *were worth* taking seriously.
- Students choose Gen Ed courses differently than other courses: they tend to look for low workloads and courses that easily deliver high grades.[2]

In short, students do not value general education because they do not think it really matters. This finding explains the surprisingly few studies in recent decades seeking to understand student perceptions of general education.[3]

Students are not alone. Indeed, general education has had harsh scholarly critics throughout its history. Writing about the general education experiment in the first part of the twentieth century, Frederick Rudolph observed, "Distribution, liberal culture, and general education all were characterized by an embarrassing lack of authority and an absence of agreement on the knowledge that should define an educated person."[4] In the latter half of the twentieth century, Hugh Hawkins called general education "an idea in distress" and "a disaster area."[5]

Although there are many reasons to consider general education a disaster area, this chapter focuses on its ethical failures. Accordingly, it makes the case that the ethical failures stem from outmoded ways of thinking about general education, the failure to connect the moral aims that originally animated the general education curriculum to a complex understanding of fundamental identity, and the marginalization of moral discourse in the academy. All these problems indicate a failure to match the actual content of general education to the moral ends used to justify it. This failure continues today with few exceptions.

THE MORAL PURPOSES OF GENERAL EDUCATION

Curricular battles always pertain to some implicit vision of human flourishing. Consider one of the first major American curricular battles in the 1800s. Charles Eliot introduced the elective system to Harvard in the late 1800s. Instead of an entirely set and required curriculum, students only had to take a first-year English course and a language.[6] To defend the innovation, Eliot made a conflicted moral argument for his elective system that was directly related to the moral formation of students.

On one hand, Eliot maintained "that the temperament, physical constitution, mental aptitudes, and moral quality of a boy are all well determined by the time he is eighteen years old."[7] Yet Eliot still also believed that the elective system provided a form of moral education during college that could change students by "impos[ing] on each individual the responsibility of forming his own habits and guiding his own conduct."[8]

This latter argument related to Eliot's desire to do away with in loco parentis, an idea he considered an ancient fiction; no American college could claim to have a discipline system perfect enough to suppress vice (apparently, he thought parents did). Of course, his system, he claimed, would come the closest. Like a clever salesperson, Eliot maintained his view that the elective system does not functionally require the college to enact parental or monastic discipline over students. Instead, he suggested that it—almost magically—trains students to govern themselves. He closed his argument with a clear moral purpose to guide educational leaders that most any clear-sighted administrator would find laughable:

> The moral purpose of a university policy should be to train young men to self-control and self-reliance through liberty. . . . Let no one imagine that that a young man is in peculiar moral danger at an active and interesting university. Far from it. Such a university is the safest place in the world for young men who

have anything in them. . . . The student lives in a bracing atmosphere; books engage him; good companionships invite him; good occupations defend him; helpful friends surround him; pure ideals are held before him; ambition spurs him; honor beckons him.[9]

One wonders if Eliot ever spent time in students' residence halls. Infected with Emersonian fever that produced an inordinate faith in self-reliance, he thought that navigating the elective system would prompt students to develop the key virtues needed for democracy.

Not surprising to any professor who has given a vague assignment, students were uncomfortable with this type of freedom. They wanted more guidance. For instance, one University of California student lamented in 1903, "All these studies were simply separate tasks that bore no definite intrinsic relation to each other. . . . The right studies were there; what was lacking was the conscious organization of them for the student."[10] Rather than an opportunity to choose, this student and others like him still asked for what professors are paid to do—teach, guide, and mentor students.

Educational leaders drew upon a new focus on academic specialization, described in the previous chapter, to help with this curricular explosion and the resulting need to help students find some organization. Since students could no longer learn the basics about every field and the elective system proved too unwieldy and chaotic for their grasp, higher education leaders developed the concept of the major. First used as a term in the in the 1877–1878 catalog of Johns Hopkins University, the idea took hold from 1910 onward as a way of helping focus students' studies.[11]

Although the major helped focus students within one area of knowledge, it provided no answer for how to orient them to knowledge outside of their specialization. As Frederick Rudolph summarized the angst of the time, "The broad synthesizing role of the curriculum, the regard for qualities of character and judgment and responsible social leadership, were being lost in the pursuit of often mundane realities of great importance for scholars and careers but of no more than marginal relevance to the history of Western ideals."[12]

The ever pragmatic John Dewey suggested simply one survey course "of the universe in its manifold phases from which a student can get an 'orientation' to the larger world."[13] More realistic suggestions tended to narrow the scope of knowledge to the great themes or books of Western civilization, such as Columbia University's Contemporary Civilizations course or various great texts proposals such as that set forth by Robert Hutchins at the University of Chicago.[14] Most institutions tried some combination of general education and majors with some electives.

The result was neither consistent nor praiseworthy. Writing in 1934, Walter Crosby Eells noted that higher education had "a curriculum that is a mass of inherited rubbish," since it was "serving as everything from a reformatory to an amusement park."[15] In most cases, the proposed general education reforms tried to encompass the development of those parts of one's humanity that went beyond being a good professional disciplinarian (e.g., biologist, historian, or psychologist).[16] In all cases, administrators and faculty alike believed general education was meant to include a moral component pertaining to the whole of a student's life.

To take a specific example, the 1945 Harvard Report on General Education noted general education "is used to indicate that part of student's whole education which looks first of all to his life as a responsible human being and citizen."[17] Conceived in this way, general education supposedly equipped students morally for the good life—for being responsible human beings.

Surveying the Moral Purposes

In their 1981 essay, *A Quest for Common Learning*, Ernest Boyer and Arthur Levine set forth in an appendix the various purposes ascribed to general education during three periods of the twentieth century when general education was emphasized (after World War I, after World War II, and during the 1970s and 1980s). Although some of the purposes were particular to each period of history, several purposes received attention during all three time periods.

These enduring purposes fit into the following categories that reflect particular identities implicitly deemed important:[18]

Our Common Humanity

- Sharing Humankind's Common Heritage
- Enhancing Global Perspectives

Democratic Identity

- Preserving a Democratic Society
- Overcoming Anti-Democratic Behavior

Ethical Identity

- Developing Moral Responsibility
- Making Commitment to Moral and Ethical Behavior
- Avoiding Unethical and Immoral Behavior
- Reducing Asocial Behavior (e.g., selfishness)
- Integrating Diverse Groups into Larger Society

Boyer and Levine also reiterated their agreement with these moral purposes. They proclaimed that the general moral purpose of general education "is to help students understand that they are not autonomous individuals, but also members of a human community to which they are accountable."[19] Overall, general education was meant, as one scholar of Boyer and Levine's time put it, to rescue us from "relativistic slough."[20]

Yet as these examples reveal, higher education leaders had a difficult time thinking in complex ethical ways about the different moral dimensions of our humanity. The justifications offered for general education focused either upon our broad humanity, our identity as a citizen, and/or our general moral identity as an individual. Little attention was given to students' other identities: family members, friends, neighbors, members of a race or gender, and more.

How then did these leaders think general education should accomplish its moral purposes? Through voluntary distribution requirements, required distribution requirements, smorgasbord requirements, core curriculum, and more, it provided students familiarity with a scattering of subjects. Hardly anyone has found this approach satisfactory.

Writing in 1971, the British scholar Eric Ashby noted that the clearest difference between American and British education was the emphasis upon general education. In his view, "It was a courageous concept: to introduce the undergraduate to the rudiments of the whole of man's intellectual heritage through surveys or selected episodes of thought. But it does not appear to have succeeded . . . for it provides information without understanding, and this is liable to destroy a student's intellectual self-confidence."[21]

A little more than a decade later, Boyer and Levine made a similar critique, "Most prescribed distributions define the purposes so broadly and permit so many different and unrelated courses to satisfy requirements, that again, no sense of commonality emerges."[22] Yet they were not enamored with the idea of a core curriculum either, stating, "Many core curricula are too narrowly focused and fail to explore the broader human relationships"[23]

Thus, Boyer and Levine concluded:

> In both purpose and practice, general education is now confused. In terms of content, there is a tendency to restrict general education to a study of specialized courses or to randomly selected themes. As to process, there is a tendency to define the options for study so broadly that no meaning can be found. With regard to outcome, there is a tendency to confuse general and liberal education and convert broadly stated goals into narrow requirements. Means and ends become confused.[24]

Consequently, they maintained that the 1977 Carnegie report conclusion that general education is a "disaster area" still held.

Indeed, those familiar with higher education know that the current imple-
mentation of general education has failed to achieve any significant moral
purpose. When describing "what every humanities scholar has been saying
for centuries when asked to defend their intellectual turf," Scott Alexander
noted their morally-derived claim: "The arts and humanities are there to teach
you the meaning of life and how to live." They claim, "The arts and humanities are there to teach you the meaning of life and how to live."

The reality is often different. He noted, "On the other hand, I've been in
humanities classes. Dozens of them, really. They were never about that. They
were about "explain how the depiction of whaling in Moby Dick sheds light
on the economic transformation of the 19th century, giving three examples
from the text. Ten pages, single spaced."[25] Can this moral mess be rescued?

Citizenship Plus Individual Capacity Acquisition

Numerous efforts to reform general education have been proposed in the last
three decades. Although some scholars proposed efforts to save an approach
that focused on a common body of knowledge, the current tendency has been
a shift toward equipping students with a certain set of capacities.[26] The results
in all the cases reveal that ethics has shifted from being an overall purpose to
being a segment of knowledge—an individual capacity in which one becomes
proficient.

For instance, one of the last efforts to save an approach to general education based on common knowledge came from Boyer and Levine. Rather
than focus on a controversial canon of great texts or set of themes that might
seem too "Western," they tried to focus upon those shared experiences
that strengthen the common bonds of humans, increase quality of life, and
enhance human relationships. "In short, [general education] should concen-
trate on those experiences that knit isolated individuals into a community."[27]

They identified what they saw as six common educational subjects that
would help with this end: 1) our shared use of symbols; 2) shared membership in groups and institutions; 3) shared producing and consuming; 4) shared
relationship with nature; 5) shared sense of time; and 6) shared values and
beliefs. Of course, the oddity of this list is that although Boyer and Levine
had wanted to emphasize the general moral purpose of general education,
they placed it last.

In general, Boyer and Levine's approach has largely disappeared in recent
decades in favor of the capacities approach. Focusing on capacities had
the advantage of shifting the focus from having to name particular ends to
only having to name capacities that might help one reach an end of one's
choice. For instance, take the favorite capacity of most every administrator:

critical thinking. Former Harvard president Derek Bok in his book, *Our Underachieving Colleges*, set forth preparation for citizenship as one of the two identity-related goals of higher education, by which he largely means national citizenship (the other identity-related goal had to do with preparation for a career accomplished through a major).[28]

In the rest of the book, Bok primarily understood humans as individuals with various capacities. The job of the individual, in this view, is what certain American authors call self-authorship.[29] Individuals are responsible for planning and building themselves, their identities, their stories, and their purposes in life. The fundamental job of the university, then, is to give individuals tools to help with that building. Bok thus largely defined the job of universities in terms of helping students develop six capacities, or tools, for building: 1) learning to communicate; 2) learning to think; 3) living with diversity; 4) preparing for a global society; 5) acquiring broader interests, and interestingly, 6) building character. Again, one finds the moral dimension is largely sequestered into one area.

One recent proposal has tried to be more overt about the universities' moral vision. Some authors affiliated with the Carnegie Foundation for the Advancement of Teaching tried to discuss general education in light of moral issues once again. Yet in their book, *Educating Citizens*, they basically took the same approach as Bok and Boyer and Levine.

They described general education largely in academic terms, identifying its role as providing "some grounding in various disciplinary approaches and methodologies and an introduction to bodies of knowledge associated with different academic fields, especially in the liberal arts and sciences."[30] They also used the "capacities" language that is common among accrediting agencies and educational administrators:

> It is expected to introduce students to the intellectual capacities needed for success in college, to provide experience with a range of options related to choosing a major, and at least in some configurations, to instill cross-cutting or higher-order skills and habits of mind, such as critical and independent thinking and both quantitative and verbal literacies.[31]

Despite sharing an approach with Bok, Boyer, and Levine, ethical ends were surprisingly absent from this description.

Ethical analysis was also absent from the authors' evaluation of means. When discussing how moral issues relate to general education, they basically described the same general education options as Boyer and Levine (e.g., distribution requirements, distribution requirements that meet explicit criteria, core curricula, comprehensive core curricula, required courses, etc.).

Only after did they discuss how ethics courses, objectives, or content might fit into these various structures. For example, they noted how in one writing requirement at Duke University, students could choose from sections focusing on ethical issues related to public health, race, technology, privacy, crime, environmentalism, and celebrity culture.

The problem with this conservative approach is that it tries to fit moral education into the current structures of the academy when a more revolutionary approach would prove beneficial. As a result, the remainder of this chapter argues that considering general education in light of a larger vision of human flourishing—one that moves beyond platitudes and vague generalities—necessitate a moral evaluation of the purposes of general education and the structure by which it is delivered.

THE PROBLEMS WITH GENERAL EDUCATION AND TWO FAILED SOLUTIONS

As one can see, past approaches to general education have tried to find commonality in two areas. They have either tried to find a common set of human knowledge or a common set of human capacities necessary for any educated person. There are major problems with both approaches.

A Common Set of Human Knowledge

The vast explosion of both knowledge and disciplines makes finding a set of common knowledge a Herculean task. Various classifications of fields of knowledge place the number of disciplines at over one thousand and growing.[32] Clearly, the purpose of general education cannot be an attempt at giving students a sampling of all disciplinary methods and knowledge. There are far too many disciplines, disciplinary methods, and knowledge for such an approach.

As a result, any attempt to choose a curriculum must rely on some moral criteria for why certain knowledge or disciplinary frameworks are chosen over others. Unfortunately, these moral criteria are not always made clear in general education frameworks. For example, Boyer and Levine try their best to identify some common areas of knowledge that are not necessarily bound by discipline. Yet, Boyer and Levine leave the moral element to the end instead of making it obvious from the start.

To avoid making their moral criteria explicit, Boyer and Levine remain vague and broad in their proposal. Thus, in suggesting that students study shared membership in groups and institutions, they recommend a course that looks "at the origin of institutions; how they evolve, grow strong, become oppressive or weak, and sometimes die."[33] They also suggest an inductive approach that looks at one institution over the course of the class such as "the Peace Corps, the AFL-CIO, the National Rifle Association, the city council."[34]

Looking at this list, it is easy to imagine how educators with particular worldviews might focus their energies. The listed topics do not appeal to human nature or natural law. Instead, they appeal to a core common human experience that apparently teaches something that has a certain generalizability.

Ultimately, this approach has trouble identifying a basic moral order that could guide any discussion of the good for the sake of moving beyond relativistic slough. Usually, one finds behind the various proposals a combination of nationalism and a longing to focus on great conversations of the past.

A few approaches have sought to draw upon and combine a whole variety of traditions. For instance, the 1945 Harvard statement proclaimed that belief in the dignity and moral responsibility of humanity "is the fruit at once of religion, of the Western tradition, and of the American tradition. It equally inspires the faith in human reason which is the basis for trust in the future of the democracy. And if it is not, strictly speaking, implied in all statements of the scientific method, there is no doubt that science has become its powerful instrument."[35]

The vision of the good that they took from this combination of traditions involved a tension regarding our ethical knowledge of the good. The statement declared in Deweyan fashion:

If you know the good, why do you seek it? If you are ignorant of the good, how do you recognize it when you find it? You must evidently at one and the same time both know it and be ignorant of it. Just so, the tradition which has come down to us regarding the nature of man and the good society must inevitably provide our standard of good. Yet an axiom of that tradition itself is the belief that no current form of the received ideal is final but that every generation, indeed every individual, must discover it in a fresh form. Education can therefore be wholly devoted neither to tradition nor to experiment, neither to the belief that the ideal in itself is enough nor to the view that means are valuable apart from the ideal. It must uphold at the same time tradition and experiment, the ideal and the means, subserving, like our culture itself, change within commitment.[36]

Being committed to the mixed tradition of preserving and finding moral change is not exactly the most stable of traditions for general education, nor does it provide any protection against moral sloth.

Additionally, these approaches to general education are all too general regarding our common humanity. Yes, we share a common humanity, but we also share specific categories of identities in which we seek to achieve excellence. Yet rarely are appeals made to *this* commonality. To illustrate, Boyer and Levine largely emphasized the tension between individualism and the community instead of understanding the tension as more complex—consisting of potential conflicts between all of our various identities as friends, lovers, family members, stewards of resources (both natural and cultural), stewards of our bodies, professionals, citizens, members of races or genders and more.

Broken down in this way, a fundamental problem with virtually every version of general education utilizing a common knowledge approach is apparent. General education in the past failed and, as it currently exists in most institutions today, still fails to equip students to think *in specific ways* about the good life as it relates to their various identities. Students take classes about marriage and family, the constitution, or health where they are provided basic knowledge; even so, the moral pursuit of excellence—that which is required for a good marriage, a good family, a good citizen, or a good steward of your body—is not at the center of the course.

The only identities relevant for moral consideration according to prevailing general education are those of the individual self, citizenship, and humanity. The fact that we are friends; family members; stewards of our bodies and resources; members of religious, social, or other communities and more is neglected.

Because of this limited view of pertinent identities, those that support these prevailing notions of general education must assume that students can easily transfer knowledge, including moral knowledge, between identity domains. If one learns honesty and courage as a student, it will easily transfer to the family, work, public life, civil society, and other identity contexts.

The reality, of course, is that scholars find this transfer of knowledge from one domain to another is one of the most difficult skills to learn.[37] As discussed in part I, learning excellence, such as the virtue of love, in one identity context (e.g., love for a spouse) does not mean that element will easily translate into another identity context (e.g., love for a neighbor). In other words, educators must consider what psychologists have "discovered" and what most people implicitly recognize: highly contextualized behavior does not often exhibit what scholars call cross-situational stability—consistency when living out different identities.[38]

Thus, loves must be ordered and identities prioritized. In fact, almost all moral conflict boils down to a conflict between two or more of identities. Can someone really be a student-athlete? Can you be a good citizen as well as a pacifist? Since the dawn of humanity, people have continuously struggled with, and will continue to struggle with, these conflicts. Unfortunately, general education based on a common set of human knowledge does an insufficient job of preparing students for these inevitable conflicts.

A Bundle of Capacities

As a result of the difficulties with the common knowledge approach in a time when knowledge is exploding, some universities operate with the understanding of students primarily as individuals with various capacities. Of course, this approach faces some of the same critiques as the earlier approach.

First, it places moral issues as a separate category and then fails to make its moral agenda explicit. Subsequently, it fails to recognize that capacities are not easily transferable. Critical thinking about art is much different than critical thinking about democracy. Eric Ericsson observed that the capacities any expert acquires are domain specific:

> You don't train to become an athlete; you train to become a gymnast or a sprinter or a marathoner or a swimmer or a basketball player. You don't train to become a doctor; you train to become a diagnostician or a pathologist or a neurosurgeon. Of course, some people do become . . . athletes in a number of sports or doctors with a general set of skills, but they do so by training a number of different areas.[39]

The same things prove true when a professor educates students in general education.

Finally, there is a problem with simply focusing upon supplying instruction to help students acquire tools for building their lives. Decrying this kind of limited approach, Arthur Holmes noted, "It does nothing to unify a person or his view of life, and it might well encourage the view that life has no overall meaning at all. It simply creates a connoisseur of the fragments of life. But a jack of all trades is a master of none, a fragmented education."[40] There is little that brings the competencies together into a coherent whole or a beautiful life structure. Though a philosophy or biology class taken here or there by a few students may address some profound questions related to personhood, such courses are very rarely linked to others in any meaningful way.

One American scholar has claimed, in response to lacking coherence in the curriculum, that every course becomes an introductory course.[41] There is no logical progression or coherence in the curriculum, particularly with regard to questions of what it means to be a flourishing human being. No wonder some recent scholars suggest we could do away with the traditional degree and its assumption of coherence and just reward students microcredentials.[42] After all, if all we want is for students to learn how to use a whole range of tools, why not just give them a microcredential that demonstrates the capacity to use a particular tool?

Of course, this approach is ultimately not how universities operate. If hoping to give someone the best tools for building something, it helps to know what they plan to build and why. Learning to draw in order to illustrate a children's book is very different than learning to draw to illustrate a textbook on anatomy. In truth, if the university is providing tools for building the self, then it follows that the university already has some implicit idea of what a well-built self entails. After all, most universities pick what competencies and virtues they think students should acquire, almost always presenting some components of the vision of the kind of self they are hoping to help students build.

If there is something that holds all these competencies together in America, it is the goal identified by Columbia University's Andrew Delbanco in *College: What It Was, Is, and Should Be*. He suggests that universities should contribute to the student's life-long pursuit of happiness.[43] American students, not surprisingly, reflect this outlook, which is implicitly communicated by the university.

Gallup recently administered a national survey to determine American college students' purposes. Reviewing responses from more than 2,500 students revealed that the top purpose students identified was to "be happy."[44] Over four-fifths (81 percent) strongly agreed that this was their highest purpose. It beat the next closest purpose by eleven percentage points. In contrast, loving God received only 38 percent support, and serving country or community received only 35 percent support.

Unfortunately, the problem with identifying happiness as a unifying purpose is that it does not prove helpful when choosing among competing loves and identities—a core process to figuring out the good life. American sociologist Robert Bellah described the problem in this way, "If selves are defined by their preferences, but those preferences are arbitrary then each self constitutes its own moral universe, and there is finally no way to reconcile conflicting claims about what is good in itself."[45]

After all, our various identities, and the competencies we use to enhance them, will inevitably compete. In building the good life, one must make decisions about which structure to design. Students, however, receive little instruction about how to use the tools they receive to make this decision. They are merely encouraged to gain competencies that will help them choose.

The ultimate problem with this competencies approach, however, is that it simply does not work. Jason Brennan and Phillip Magness illustrate this point by using the example of required general education English composition classes.[46] Their overview of the research found that there is little evidence that these classes actually help students improve their writing and gain this particular competency. However, evidence exists that these classes provide work for an oversaturated English PhD market and increase student enrollment and retention patterns. The same proves true with foreign language courses, which Brennan and Magness found do not help students speak a foreign language but instead helped supply faculty with jobs.[47]

Overall, Brennan and Magness argue that a capacities approach to general education results in the following immoral scenario, "Faculty exploit students for their own selfish benefit, although they disguise this practice with moralistic arguments. . . . [G]eneral education requirements for undergraduates are a form of academic rent-seeking. Their purpose is *not* really to give students breadth, make them well-rounded, or introduce them to new areas of research. Their real purpose is to line professors' pockets at students' expense."[48]

By rent-seeker, the authors mean, someone "who uses a political process— as opposed to supplying a productive service—to obtain, extend, and preserve the flow of income or other benefits to him or herself at others' expense."[49] The cost, which may be as high as $26,000, is then transferred to the student or the taxpayer who must pay for ineffectual but required courses. As a result, Brennan and Magness claim current general education, although justified using moral arguments, actually is immoral in its results.

General education simply forces students to do something that is not for the public good or the students' good, but the professors' good. Even worse, "Professors have a stake in gaming gen eds for their own benefit. They have a selfish incentive to manipulate gen ed requirements to force students to take their classes. Furthermore, they may even have a perverse incentive to ensure their skills classes *don't work*, in order to justify forcing students to take additional classes" (e.g., two instead of one semester of freshman comp).[50] In light of this moral disaster, is general education even worth saving?

Giving Up

Given the two-faced nature of general education, its moral inconsistency, its ineffectiveness, and its general disconnect from its lofty moral aims, it is no surprise that some suggest giving up. Zachary Michael Jack argued that any Gen Ed revision should be a Gen Ed reduction.[51]

He also claimed that at many institutions, the cost to take general education requirements is enormous, perhaps $50,000 in a private university requiring a mere forty hours of general education. He maintained that, in light of the student debt crisis, extensive general education requirements can no longer be morally justified. If general education remains as is, Jack's assessment is valid and the implications severe. In the absence of a general education revolution, the current approach to general education is no longer justifiable.

LEADING THE REVOLUTION: TEACHING THE GREAT IDENTITIES

In light of the explosion of knowledge, disciplines, and disciplinary methods, educators can no longer pretend to provide a general education. What then can be provided? Arriving at a conclusion requires exploring one simple question: Who are we? This is the most important moral question facing undergraduates today. Only in knowing who we are, can we discern our telos, what we ought to pursue.[52]

In his book *What Is a Person*, Christian Smith, a sociologist at the University of Notre Dame, rhetorically asks and answers: "What are humans? One would think that of all the personal and scientific subjects we study the one we would be the most interested and proficient in understanding would be ourselves, human beings."[53] One would think.

Yet the reality that secular universities in North America often fail to prioritize or even address this matter adequately remains. As C. John Sommerville wrote in his book, *The Decline of the Secular University*, "If there is one thing that should raise the question of the secular university's irrelevance it might especially be in the failure to justify or even make sense of the concept of the human."[54] An education in the Great Identities, which I propose in chapter 7, would correct this problem. First, however, we also need to understand the moral problems present within the rest of the curriculum and contemporary cocurricular education.

NOTES

1. Members of the Harvard University General Education Review Committee. "General Education Review Committee Interim Report." HarvardMagazine.com. (Accessed April 6, 2020). https://harvardmagazine.com/sites/default/files/FAS_Gen_Ed_Interim_Review.pdf.

2. Harvard University General Education Review Committee, "General Education Review Committee Interim Report," 3–4. For an example of past scholarship see Jerry Gaff, *Project on General Education Models: GEM Newsletter*, Washington, DC: no. 5, September 1980, 1–8.

3. S. E. Gump, "Classroom Research in a General Education Course: Exploring Implications through an Investigation of the Sophomore Slump," *Journal of General Education* 56 (2007): 105–25; D. Humphreys and A. Davenport, "What Really

Matters in College: How Students View and Value Liberal Education," *Liberal Education*, retrieved from https://www.aacu.org/liberaleducation/le-sufa05/le-sufa05leap .cfm; J. S. Johnston Jr., R. C. Reardon, G. L. Kramer, J. G. Lenz, A. S. Maduros, and J. P. Sampson Jr., "The Demand Side of General Education: Attending to Student Attitudes and Understandings," *Journal of General Education* 40 (1991): 180–200; L. O. King and J. W. Kotrlik, "Relevance of the General Education Core Curriculum to Career Goals of College of Agriculture Students," *Journal of Agricultural Education* 36 (1995): 26–33; Clarissa A. Thompson, Michele Eodice, and Phuoc Tran, "Student Perceptions of General Education Requirements at a Large Public University: No Surprises?" *The Journal of General Education* 64, no. 4 (2015): 278–93; B. A. Vander Schee, "Changing General Education Perceptions Through *Perspectives* and the Interdisciplinary First-Year Seminar," *International Journal of Teaching and Learning in Higher Education* 23 (2011): 382–87.

4. Frederick Rudolph, *Curriculum: A History of the American Undergraduate Course of Study 1636* (San Francisco: Jossey-Bass, 1977), 243.

5. Hugh Hawkins, "Curricular Reform in Historical Perspective," *Perspectives: American Historical Association Newsletter* 24, no. 1 (January 1986): 21–23.

6. See W. B. Carnochan, *The Battleground of the Curriculum: Liberal Education and the American Experience* (Stanford, CA: Stanford University Press, 1993), 1–21.

7. Charles Eliot, *Educational Reform: Essays and Addresses* (New York: The Century Co. 1898), 131.

8. Eliot, *Educational Reform*, 125.

9. Eliot, *Educational Reform*, 148.

10. Laurence R. Veysey, *The Emergence of the American University* (Chicago: University of Chicago Press, 1965), 114.

11. James L. Ratcliff, "Academic Major, The," *Encyclopedia of Education*, edited by James W. Guthrie, 2nd ed. (New York: Macmillan Reference, 2003), 1:19–23; Rudolph, *Curriculum.*

12. Rudolph, *Curriculum,* 243.

13. Russell Thomas, *The Search for a Common Learning* (New York, McGraw-Hill, 1963), 52–53.

14. See W. B. Carnochan, *The Battleground of the Curriculum: Liberal Education and the American Experience* (Stanford, CA: Stanford University Press, 1993), 68–87.

15. Walter Crosby Eells, "Criticisms of Higher Education," *The Journal of Higher Education* 5, no. 4 (1934): 187–89.

16. Ernest L. Boyer and Arthur Levine defined general education as "the learning that should be common to all people." Yet if there is that learning should be common to all people, it should be required of everyone in high school. Of course, there were others in the whole general education conversation who are fine being a bit snobby. One scholar noted of general education programs, "Such programs all seek to identify among the vast ranges of human knowledge those *fundamentals* essential to the well-being of *cultivated* men" (Mayhew, "General Education," 62, italics mine). Apparently, college educated men (and women) were to be distinguished by being more cultivated.

17. Harvard Committee, "General Education in a Free Society" (Harvard University, 1945), 17.

18. Ernest L. Boyer and Arthur Levine, *A Quest for Common Learning* (Washington, DC: The Carnegie Foundation for the Advancement of Teaching, 1981), 59–60.

19. Boyer and Levine, *A Quest for Common Learning*, 22.

20. Martin Kaplan, "The Wrong Solution to the Right Problem," in *In Opposition to Core Curriculum: Alternative Models for Undergraduate Education*, ed. James W. Hall with B. L. Kevles (Westport, CT: Greenwood Press, 1982), 7.

21. Eric Ashby, *Any Person, Any Study: An Essay on Higher Education in the United States* (New York: McGraw-Hill Book Co., 1971), 34.

22. Boyer and Levine, *A Quest for Common Learning*, 31.

23. Boyer and Levine, *A Quest for Common Learning*, 31.

24. Boyer and Levine, *A Quest for Common Learning*, 33.

25. Scott Alexander, "Book Review: Twelve Rules for Life," SlateStarCodex.com, accessed April 10, 2020, http://slatestarcodex.com/2018/03/26/book-review-twelve-rules-for-life/.

26. Sandra Logan and Madeline Shellgren, "Deliberative Democracy as an End without Means: From Experience-based to Competency-based Pedagogies in Support of Transformative Learning," *The Journal of General Education* 68, no. 1–2 (2019): 32–53.

27. Boyer and Levine, *A Quest for Common Learning*, 35.

28. Derek Bok, *Our Underachieving Colleges: A Candid Look at How Much Students Learn and Why They Should Be Learning More* (Princeton, NJ: Princeton University Press, 2006), 67–81.

29. Marcia B. Baxter Magolda, *Making Their Own Way: Narratives for Transforming Higher Education to Promote Self-Development* (Sterling, VA: Stylus Press, 2001); Marcia B. Baxter Magolda, *Creating Contexts for Learning and Self-Authorship: Constructive-Developmental Pedagogy* (Nashville, TN: Vanderbilt University Press, 1999); Marcia B. Baxter Magolda and Patricia M. King, *Theories and Models of Practice to Educate for Self-Authorship* (Sterling, VA: Stylus, 2004). See also Robert J. Nash and Michelle C. Murray, *Helping College Students Find Purpose: The Campus Guide to Meaning-Making* (San Francisco: Jossey-Bass, 2010).

30. Anne Colby, Thomas Ehrlich, Elizabeth Beaumont, and Jason Stephens, *Educating Citizens: Preparing America's Undergraduates for Lives of Moral and Civic Responsibility* (San Francisco: Jossey-Bass, 2003), 170.

31. Colby et al., *Educating Citizens*, 170.

32. See for example the United Kingdom's Higher Education Classification of Subjects, https://www.hesa.ac.uk/innovation/hecos or the National Center for Education Statistics Classification, https://nces.ed.gov/pubs2002/cip2000/.

33. Boyer and Levine, *A Quest for Common Learning*, 38.

34. Boyer and Levine, *A Quest for Common Learning*, 38.

35. Wilson Smith and Thomas Bender, *American Higher Education Transformed, 1940–2005: Documenting the National Discourse* (Baltimore, MD: Johns Hopkins University Press, 2008); Harvard Committee, "General Education in a Free Society," 17.

36. Smith and Bender, *American Higher Education Transformed*, 17.

37. James M. Lang, *Cheating Lessons: Learning from Academic Dishonesty* (Cambridge, MA: Harvard University Press, 2013), 175–78.

38. Kwame Appiah, *Experiments in Ethics* (Cambridge, MA: Harvard University Press, 2008).

39. Anders Ericsson and Robert Pool, *Peak: Secrets from the New Science of Expertise* (New York: Houghton Mifflin Harcourt, 2016), 60.

40. Arthur Frank Holmes, *The Idea of the Christian College* (Grand Rapids, MI: Eerdmans Publishing, 1987), 27.

41. Stanley Hauerwas, "The Possibility of Christian Higher Education: A Panel Discussion," Baylor University lecture, March 17, 2016.

42. "Could Micro-credentials Compete with Traditional Degrees?" BBC, February 17, 2020, https://www.bbc.com/worklife/article/20200212-could-micro-credentials-compete-with-traditional-degrees.

43. Andrew Delbanco, *College: What It Was, Is and Should Be* (Princeton, NJ: Princeton University Press, 2012).

44. Perry L. Glanzer, Jonathan P. Hill, and Byron R. Johnson, *The Quest for Purpose: The Collegiate Search for a Meaningful Life* (Albany: State University of New York Press, 2017).

45. Robert N. Bellah, Richard Madsen, William M. Sullivan, Ann Swidler, and Steven M. Tipton, *Habits of the Heart: Individualism and Commitment in American Life* (San Francisco: Harper & Row, 1985), 80.

46. Jason Brennan and Phillip Magness, *Cracks in the Ivory Tower: The Moral Mess of Higher Education* (New York: Oxford University Press, 2019), 172.

47. In addition, they found that there is no evidence that general education helps students discover their major or encounter new academic fields. Instead of filling the first week before class with "ice cream socials or ideologically loaded reading groups led by administrators," they suggest institutions could simply offer ten different one-hour sessions that introduce students to the field; Brennan and Magness, *Cracks in the Ivory Tower*, 181.

48. Brennan and Magness, *Cracks in the Ivory Tower*, 157, 161.

49. Brennan and Magness, *Cracks in the Ivory Tower*, 161.

50. Brennan and Magness, *Cracks in the Ivory Tower*, 180.

51. Zachary Michael Jack, "Colleges Should Consider Halving Gen Ed Curriculum Requirements," *Inside Higher Education*, April 5, 2018, http://insidehighered.com/views/2018/04/05/colleges-should-consider-halving-gen-ed-curriculum-requirements-opinion.

52. Alasdair C. MacIntyre, *After Virtue: A Study in Moral Theory*, 3rd edition (South Bend, IN: University of Notre Dame Press, 2007).

53. Christian Smith, *What Is a Person? Rethinking Humanity, Social Life, and the Moral Good from the Ground Up* (Chicago: University of Chicago Press, 2010), 1.

54. C. John Sommerville, *The Decline of the Secular University* (New York: Oxford University Press, 2006), 8.

Chapter 5

The Curricular Reduction of Ethics to Professional Ethics

[T]he liberal arts institutions have attempted to become what they should not really be. . . . Instead of remaining the makers of men [*sic*], they have become the makers of workers and of knowledge. They have to a large extent abandoned their ancient and honorable task of training young people to live informed, intelligent, and integrated lives. They seem to have forgotten the admonition of Montaigne that "the object of education is to make, not a scholar, but a man [*sic*]."

—Earl J. McGrath, 1959[1]

Outside of general education, faculty are responsible for teaching their students excellence in particular professional identities (e.g., being an excellent accountant, biologist, historian, social worker, etc.). In this regard, becoming an excellent professional is necessarily a moral endeavor. Michael Davis, a specialist in professional ethics, provides a helpful definition of a profession that amplifies this point: "A profession is a number of individuals in the same occupation voluntarily organized to earn a living by openly serving a certain moral ideal in a morally-permissible way beyond what law, market, and morality would otherwise require."[2] Said another way, professionals necessarily require some sort of moral tradition for their professional practice to function, and students must be inculcated into this tradition.

Professional ethics education first originated with the creation of the professions and professional ethics codes between 1890 and 1920.[3] It largely disappeared, however, due to the rise of logical positivism, modernism, and the social scientific emphasis on separating facts and values.[4] Nonetheless, by the 1970s, contemporary professionals realized how unprepared they were to address a plethora of new ethical dilemmas brought about by advancements in technology. Medical professionals needed ethics courses to help them navigate the difficult decisions regarding organ transplants, in-vitro fertilization, and more.[5] Furthermore, legal and business crises also produced a demand for greater attention to ethics.[6] Consequently, professional ethics made a comeback.

The first modern medical ethics text was published in 1976.[7] Soon, professional ethics courses began to blossom once again in law, business, and other professions. By 1979, the Hasting Center found that half of institutions with ethics courses had courses in applied ethics (e.g., "bioethics, business ethics, the morality of war, or ethics and human experimentation").[8] It concluded, "There has been a resurgence of teaching ethics at the college level."[9]

This new ethics boom almost always approached ethics from a philosophical vantage point, tending to focus upon a few broad principles or virtues. For instance, medical ethics students were encouraged to examine moral dilemmas in light of the supposedly common virtues of beneficence, non-maleficence, autonomy, and justice, which could—in theory—be defined, understood, and embraced apart from any metaphysical or theological narrative.[10] Students were then encouraged to focus upon rationally resolving particular moral dilemmas in light of these broad principles.

If different moral traditions were addressed, they usually fell within two general philosophical schools of thought: utilitarianism and Kantian ethics. Religion was largely ignored. In fact, professional ethics in many ways took the functional place of religion in the curriculum. Bruce Wilshire even claimed in *The Moral Collapse of the University*, "Professionalism emerges as a quasi-religion, our only way, apparently, of holding ourselves together after the disintegration of religious myths and pre-industrial traditions."[11] Yet, unlike most religions, the ethical guidance upon which professional ethics relied was devoid of any metaphysical connection to the broader human identity or story.

THE NATURE AND LIMITS OF CONTEMPORARY PROFESSIONAL ETHICS

Today, this professional moral tradition continues to dominate higher education. Virtually every college major associated with a professional society has a code of ethics and texts addressing professional ethics. Perusing these texts and codes reveals that they are still primarily focused upon identity excellence within the profession (e.g., "Developing a professional identity as a counselor").[12]

This siloed approach is understandable but also problematic, especially if there is no ethics education also having interidentity moral conversations with students. Neither the rest of the human person nor the rest of moral reality is significantly accounted for within these professional ethics texts. One learns to think primarily as a professional and not also as a citizen, friend, religious believer, family member, steward of the culture, caretaker of the environment, and more.

As a result of this siloed approach to identity in professional ethics, other identities and their associated ends, principles, or virtues—or perhaps, a metaidentity with their metaends, virtues, and principles—do not come into extensive play in these texts. Thus, students are given limited exposure to the range of identity conflicts (mentioned in chapter 3) that they will inevitably face within their lived experiences (what does it mean to be a good friend, parent, Muslim, caretaker of the environment, and a good businessperson?).

They will also fail to understand the conflicts between purposes, principles, or virtues associated with both the professional identity and any other identity. Moreover, students are not asked to deal extensively with identity prioritization that involves their other identities alongside their professional identity (e.g., How do I be an excellent professional and spouse, citizen, friend, etc.?).

In light of this identity focus, it is no surprise that the ends, principles, and/ or virtues evaluated are considered internal goods of the professional practice (versus a wide range of human virtues such as those identified in positive psychology). In other words, medical ethics still primarily addresses the virtues or principles of autonomy, non-maleficence, beneficence, utility, and justice while avoiding other virtues such as gentleness, kindness, forgiveness, etc.[13]

Sometimes the list expands. For example, counseling does add fidelity and veracity, but the list is still limited to professional principles/virtues.[14] The same is true with other professions. A journalist's focus is to: 1) seek truth and report it; 2) minimize harm; 3) act independently; and 4) be accountable and transparent.[15] Accountants discuss the nature of true disclosure.[16] Criminal justice, obviously, deals with justice.[17] And the list goes on.

At some point, most professional ethics texts provide students a diagram or table that illustrates the process of making an ethical decision in their profession.[18] Yet such frameworks limit identity considerations to those related to the profession. For instance, a journalist asks, "What is my journalistic purpose?" Within the ethical decision-making process presented by most texts, this question can be adequately answered without any consideration of one's larger human purpose—or other metapurposes—associated with higher priority identities.[19]

Larger ethical theories could be employed to undertake this kind of non-siloed evaluation, but this does not happen for two reasons. First, students are only exposed to philosophical and not theological approaches to ethics (e.g., Kantianism, feminist, utilitarianism, Aristotelian virtue ethics, etc. versus Christian, Jewish, Muslim ethics). Consequently, almost every professional ethics text begins by describing the three philosophical approaches to ethics, each prioritizing a different element (e.g., utilitarianism, virtue ethics, and deontological approaches to ethics). Only a few provide one or two pages to the role of "ethical decision making and religion."[20] The vast majority do not.

In this regard, professional ethics secularizes ethical thinking in a way that Warren Nord describes as typical within education: "We systematically and uncritically teach students to make sense of the world in exclusively secular categories. Consequently, the great majority of students earn . . . their undergraduate degrees without ever contending with a live religious idea."[21] If students are only exposed to secular philosophical ways of thinking they are being indoctrinated.

In fact, Nord concludes, "Students are indoctrinated when they are systematically and uncritically taught to accept one basic framework for interpreting reality over other major live alternatives"[22] Professional ethics, in most current forms, serves as a kind of secular indoctrination into a secular way of thinking about the professions by ignoring religious approaches to professional ethics that are still viable options.[23]

Furthermore, these philosophical traditions of ethics are simply employed on behalf of the profession and not with regard to other identities or life as a whole. Thus, students only learn how a Kantian, utilitarian, or feminist might reason morally within a given profession, but not in life as a whole among competing identities. In fact, students are not ever asked how they would deal with the utilitarian who gives attention to other identities beyond their professional identity, particularly when this attention is motivated simply by happiness or, perhaps, the happiness of an important social group. Instead, ethical issues are largely contained within the profession.

In sum, students are not given a liberal education about possible approaches to professional ethics at multiple levels. They are not taught how to think according to religious and philosophical theories or frameworks. They are not taught to think about their profession within their other identities, and they are not challenged to prioritize their professional identity in relationship to other identities. In many ways, students receive a form of secular philosophical indoctrination into how to be excellent in a profession. The only liberal part of the education is the exposure to standard philosophical ethical theories as applied to each profession.[24]

PROFESSIONS WITHOUT IDENTITY EXCELLENCE ELEMENTS OR A METAIDENTITY

Unfortunately, when evaluated according to the ethical framework in this book, the problem with professional ethics extends beyond these secular and indoctrinating characteristics in two important ways: reducing identity excellence to a few primary elements and disconnecting ethics from larger traditions.

Reduction and Isolation

First, most professional societies and authors of profession-based ethics texts reduce ethics to a set of three moral elements related to identity excellence within a particular identity: ends, virtues, and rules/principles. Yet these ends, virtues, and rules/principles are not accompanied by other elements of identity excellence, particularly a larger metanarrative. Additionally, they often ignore the wisdom tradition of ethics, the importance of mentors and models, and the role of moral imagination.

This tendency, especially the failure to recognize the shortcomings of situating ethics within a professional identity and professional narrative, leads to a second problem with professional ethics. It is often approached as an endeavor disconnected from larger traditions. The assumption is that the moral tradition of the profession can survive and prosper alone without deeper philosophical or religious roots.

But what happens then when a profession becomes morally limited or corrupted? How does it reform, transform, or redeem itself? Or does it ever need help from outside moral traditions? For example, the medical profession's problematic treatment of African Americans is well known, and this chapter already mentioned the reductive view of medical ethics in the mid-twentieth century.[25] What helped reform these practices?

Moral traditions external to the medical profession eventually had to supply broader views of human personhood and ethics to reform medicine's professional ethics. Unfortunately, as already mentioned in the previous chapter, students are not taught the range of moral traditions (usually a standard set of philosophical traditions). Consequently, they often lack a liberal education in moral traditions that could supplement and help reform and transform a corrupt tradition of professional ethics.

Beyond Going It Alone

In the new revival of professional ethics that occurred in the 1970s, some philosophers tried to address these problems. They recognized that perhaps there might be a time when it would be wrong for a doctor to pursue health or a lawyer the interests of their clients. How then should professionals approach these issues? Recognizing the need for a higher authority, moral philosophers in higher education turned to the only moral identity and tradition in which Americans could find some agreement—the democratic identity and tradition. In particular, philosophers sought refuge in the democratic telos of autonomy and the rights capable of preserving this autonomy in the Bill of Rights.

The justification of autonomy as the ultimate moral telos varied. Some professional ethicists turned to human dignity as the foundation. For instance, Alex Goldman, writing in his 1980 book *The Moral Foundations of Professional Ethics*, oddly claimed we must preserve

> the ability of individuals to formulate their own plans in life. The truth of relativism suggests that values originate in the distinct valuations of persons with goals and desires. If it is in relation to such freely valuing individuals and their central projects that other goods acquire their value or utility, then it makes sense that the precondition for the exercise of creative individuality and valuation should take absolute precedence. . . . There is therefore an ideal-regarding source of the priority of individual rights.[26]

Consistent with a worldview rooted in Meta-Democracy, the choice-making individual was the primary source of value that Goldman cited to support his prioritization of autonomy.

The moral tradition of Meta-Democracy has received some critique. In *Grounding Professional Ethics in a Pluralistic Society*, Paul Camenisch found Davis's approach unsatisfactory. Like Davis, Camenisch understood the professions as limited moral subcommunities committed to particular moral ideals. Yet he thought that what could provide the needed foundation or supplement to professional ethics pertained to society and not individual human dignity. He claimed regarding professions,

> They are part of society's complex set of arrangements for providing its members optimal opportunity for the fullest life possible. Thus, professional ethics must begin by looking not at some abstract conception of right, or of reason, or even of justice and health, but rather at the role the professions play or were meant to play in the society in which they function. . . . Without this foundation in a societally assigned task and societally defined goals the professions as we know them simply would not exist.[27]

Instead of the democratically-derived concept of individual autonomy supporting professional ethics, Davis maintained the abstract concept of society and the role professions play in that society should be the "foundation."

Camenisch rightly recognized that such an understanding of professions in a pluralistic society created the previously identified problem: "[A]ny moral fragmentation and uncertainty in the society itself will be reflected in the professions and their ethics."[28] Camenisch responded to this problem by claiming that the moral diversity of our society is overrated. He argued that the immediate moral responses of individuals to actual life issues supersedes any philosophical and religious theories.

This approach helps us "to free ourselves of the overly reflective and rational, even deductive model of the moral life which academic philosophy and theology have helped generate."[29] Thus, instead of looking to academic ethics, we must look to lived moral communities and the common moral consensus found between them. To some extent, as demonstrated by the success of K–12 character education and positive psychology, this strategy has had some limited usefulness and success.

The most insightful contribution that has been made to the argument that professional ethics cannot and should not survive on its own was Mike Martin's 2000 book *Meaningful Work: Rethinking Professional Ethics.* Martin took to task the one hundred-year-old "consensus paradigm" that professional ethics consists largely of duties and dilemmas that involve two parts: "(a) identifying the duties that are or should be standardized within professional codes of ethics applicable to all members of a profession, and (b) grappling with how to apply the duties to particular situations where they conflict or have unclear implications."[30]

Martin considered the "consensus paradigm" implausible and constricting, stating:

> Usually it operates as the unspoken legacy of Immanuel Kant's preoccupation with universal principles, as well as the emphasis on general rules in most human rights ethics, contract theory (which grounds morality in the rules that ideally rational agents would agree upon), and rule-utilitarianism (the view that right conduct is specified by a code of conduct that maximizes the social good).[31]

Martin pointed out that this consensus paradigm limited the influence of other moral identity traditions. For example, he argued for rethinking professional ethics in light of "personal commitments" such as family life.

Unfortunately, Martin still relied too heavily on abstract "ideals" and "values" (an ambiguous catch-all ethical term), failing to consider directly how particular identities and their associated stories help people think through the moral complexity involved with conflicts. For example, instead of understanding what it means to be a good mother or father, he identified these identities as merely "personal commitments," though they are, in fact, identities with their own historical moral traditions. Still, he understood an important point. Professional ethics cannot flourish by simply thinking about the good of professions alone.

Martin provides the best example of how this challenge works when examining the virtue of integrity. He contended that integrity requires not merely being content thinking about each identity area in one's life; but rather, showing integrity as a mother, a professional, a spouse, a citizen, and more. He wrote:

> Even more than most virtues, integrity resists fragmentation into insulated domains, as its very etymology suggests: *in-tegritas* means wholeness and suggests unity, interrelatedness, integration, harmony among aspects of character. . . . Integrity provokes us to seek wider unities. If we are to establish a framework for connecting professional with other major dimensions of life, we need to attend to a professional's wider integrity, integrity defined by professional duties and roles and much more.[32]

To make this difference clear, he delineated between *role* integrity and *overall* integrity.

For Martin, overall integrity was not achievable through the ranking of one's different identities (e.g., family always comes before work). Instead, overall integrity necessitates pragmatic moral reasoning in different contexts to determine how to order one's identities. As a result, Morris was quite content to suggest that prioritization of professional ends and virtues, as compared to familial identity and its associated ends and virtue, will vary from situation to situation.

Martin's inclusion and consideration of identities beyond professional or democratic narrative ends is promising but incomplete. It is clear that Martin believed selfishness in either identity domain is problematic and that serving others for the common good is to be praised. Yet he suggested no overarching metaidentity beyond the self as the basis for this claim.

Overall, some scholars have found the recent half-century tradition of focusing upon professional ethics wanting. Even so, replacement options are rather limited and quite general. In an increasingly pluralistic academy and the larger professions, attempts at recognizing that professionals and professions cannot be morally sustained on their own are lacking. Professionals and professions need to be guided by external moral traditions. In the pluralistic university setting, however, those connections are not encouraged or even explored.

As a result, most contemporary universities focus primarily on professional ethics, subsequently neglecting any larger identity or metaphysical metanarrative that gives meaning to one's vision for a flourishing life. Furthermore, professional ethics texts do the same. Thus, ethics is disconnected from any larger metanarrative beyond that of the profession. Of course, the limited power of this approach to transform students is revealed by the simple question: How many people have lived or died for a professional ethics code?

The Odd Outlier that Proves the Point

Notably, the profession of K–12 education is one of the odd outliers in the development of ethics education. One might think that this profession, more so than others, would give attention not only to professional ethics but also to the character education of students. Yet studies of teacher education programs' attention to ethics education—throughout the history of professional ethics—reveal that moral education—whether the professional ethics of educators or the moral education of students—is extremely limited.[33]

In other words, teacher training programs did not follow the "ethics boom" reported among other professional disciplines both in offering courses in professional ethics or in courses to help teachers engage in the moral or character education of students. Interestingly, the extensive character education movement that has emerged in K–12 education has had little influence upon the profession of teacher education.

Overall, despite its limitations, the professional moral identity, and its associated moral tradition of education, along with that of being a good liberal Democrat, have had tremendous staying power in academia. Today, they are the two major identities used to guide moral education. For example, former president of Harvard, Derek Bok, wrote a book that sets forth specific purposes for colleges, and he only uses identities to frame two: helping students become good citizens and good professionals.[34] The next chapter examines how the cocurricular dimension attempts to form good citizens.

NOTES

1. Earl I. McGrath, *The Graduate School and the Decline of Liberal Education* (New York: Teachers College, 1959), vi.

2. Michael Davis, *Profession, Code and Ethics* (Burlington, VT: Ashgate, 2002), 3. One finds a similar moral emphasis in the more convoluted definition of a profession offered by Darrell Reeck: "A profession is an occupational group which specialized in the performance of such highly developed skills for the meeting of a complex human needs that the right use of them is achieved only under the discipline of an ethic developed and enforce by peers and by mastery of a broader contextual knowledge of the nature of the human being, society, the natural world, and historical trends." Darrell Reeck, *Ethics for the Professions: A Christian Perspective* (Minneapolis, MN: Augsburg Publishing House, 1982), 30.

3. Douglas Sloan, "The Teaching of Ethics in the American Undergraduate Curriculum, 1876–1976," in *Ethics Teaching in Higher Education*, eds. Daniel Callahan and Sissela Bok (New York: Plenum Press, 1980); Julie Reuben, *The Making of the Modern University: Intellectual Transformation and the Marginalization of Morality* (Chicago: University of Chicago Press, 1996).

4. See chapter 6 in Perry L. Glanzer, *The Dismantling of Moral Education: How Higher Education Reduced the Human Identity* (Lanham, MD: Rowman & Littlefield, 2022).

5. Derek Bok, *Beyond the Ivory Tower: Social Responsibilities of the Modern University* (Cambridge, MA: Harvard University Press, 1982).

6. Bok, *Beyond the Ivory Tower.*

7. Michael Davis, *Ethics and the University* (New York: Routledge, 2002).

8. Daniel Callahan and Sissela Bok, eds., *Ethics Teaching in Higher Education* (New York: The Hastings Center, 1980), 13.

9. Callahan and Bok, *Ethics Teaching in Higher Education*, 159.

10. Thomas L. Beauchamp and James F. Childress, *Principles of Biomedical Ethics* (New York: Oxford University Press, 1979).

11. Bruce Wilshire, *The Moral Collapse of the University: Professionalism, Purity and Alienation* (Albany: State University of New York Press, 1990), 277.

12. For evidence for this section, I drew upon the following popular professional ethics texts in these different fields. Accounting: Ronald F. Duska and Brenda Shay Duska, *Accounting Ethics* (Malden, MA; Blackwell Publishing, 2003); Bioethics: Lewis Vaughn, *Bioethics: Principles, Issues, and Cases*, 4th ed. (New York: Oxford University Press, 2020); James F. Childress and Tom L. Beauchamp, *Principles of Biomedical Ethics,* 7th ed. (New York: Oxford University Press, 2013); Business: O. C. Ferrell, John Fraedrich, and Linda Ferrell, *Business Ethics: Ethical Decision Making and Cases*, 12th ed. (Boston: Cengage, 2019); William H. Shaw, *Business Ethics*, 9th ed. (Boston: Cengage, 2017); Linda Klebe Treviño and Katherine A. Nelson *Managing Business Ethics: Straight Talk about How to Do It Right*, 6th ed. (San Francisco: Wiley, 2014); Counseling: Theodore P. Remley Jr. and Barbara Herlihy, *Ethical, Legal, and Professional Issues in Counseling*, 6th ed. (Boston: Pearson, 2020); Criminal Justice: Jay S. Albanese, *Professional Ethics in Criminal Justice: Being Ethical when No One Is Looking*, 4th ed. (Boston: Pearson, 2016); Engineering: Charles E. Harris Jr., Michael S. Pritchard, Ray W. James, Elaine E. Englehardt, and Michael J. Rabins, *Engineering Ethics: Concepts and Cases* (Boston: Cengage, 2019); Martin Peterson, *Ethics for Engineers* (New York: Oxford University Press, 2020); General Professional Ethics: Alex H. Goldman, *The Moral Foundations of Professional Ethics* (Totowa, NJ: Rowman & Littlefield, 1980); Clancy Martin, Wayne Vaught, and Robert C. Solomon, *Ethics Across the Professions: A Reader for Professional Ethics* (New York: Oxford University Press, 2010); Helping Professions: Gearld Corey, Cindy Corey, Marianne Schneider Corey, and Patrick Callanan, *Issues and Ethics in the Helping Professions*, 9th ed. (Boston: Cengage, 2015); Information Technology: George W. Reynolds, *Ethics in Information Technology*, 6th ed. (Boston: Cengage, 2019); Journalism: Gene Foreman, *The Ethical Journalist: Making Responsible Decisions in the Digital Age*, 2nd ed. (Malden, MA: Wiley Blackwell, 2016); Media Ethics: Lee Anne Peck and Guy S. Reel, *Media Ethics at Work: True Stories from Young Professionals*, 2nd ed. (Thousand Oaks, CA: Sage Publications, 2017); Social Work: Allan Edward Barsky, *Ethics and Values in Social Work: An Integrated Approach for a Comprehensive Curriculum* (New York: Oxford University Press, 2019).

13. See Beauchamp and Childress, *Principles of Biomedical Ethics*; Vaughn, *Bioethics.*

14. Remley and Herlihy, *Ethical, Legal, and Professional Issues in Counseling.*

15. Foreman, *The Ethical Journalist*, 89.

16. Duska and Duska, *Accounting Ethics.*

17. Albanese, *Professional Ethics in Criminal Justice.*

18. Duska and Duska, *Accounting Ethics*, 35–41; Ferrell, Fraedrich, and Ferrell, *Business Ethics*, 116; Foreman, *The Ethical Journalist*, 118; Reynolds, *Ethics in Information Technology*, 24–27.

19. Foreman, *The Ethical Journalist*, 118.

20. See for example Peck and Reel, *Media Ethics at Work*, 20; Vaughn, *Bioethics.*

21. Warren A. Nord, *Does God Make a Difference? Taking Religion Seriously in Our Schools and Universities* (Oxford: Oxford University Press, 2010), 5.

22. Nord, *Does God Make a Difference?*, 92.

23. See as examples: Michael E. Cafferky, *Business Ethics in Biblical Perspective: A Comprehensive Introduction* (Downers Grove, IL: IVP Academic, 2015); C. Ben Mitchell and D. Joy Riley, *Christian Bioethics: A Guide for Pastors, Health Care Professionals, and Families* (Nashville, TN: B & H Academic, 2014); Randolph K. Sanders, *Christian Counseling Ethics: A Handbook for Psychologists, Therapists and Pastors*, 2nd ed. (Downers Grove, IL: IVP Academic, 2013); Richard B. Steel and Heidi A. Monroe, *Christian Ethics and Nursing Practice* (Portland, OR: Cascade Publishing, 2020); Terry A. Wolfer and Cheryl Brandsen, *Virtues and Character in Social Work Practice* (Botsford, CT: North American Association of Christians in Social Work, 2015); Kenman L. Wong and Scott B. Rae, *Business for the Common Good: A Christian Vision for the Marketplace* (Downers Grove, IL: Intervarsity Press, 2011).

24. Perry L. Glanzer, *The Dismantling of Moral Education: How Higher Education Reduced the Human Identity* (Lanham, MD: Rowman & Littlefield, 2022).

25. James H. Jones, *Bad Blood: the Tuskegee Syphilis Experiment* (New York: Free Press, 1981).

26. Goldman, *The Moral Foundations of Professional Ethics*, 27–28.

27. Paul Camenisch, *Grounding Professional Ethics in a Pluralistic Society* (New York: Haven, 1983), 55–56.

28. Camenisch, *Grounding Professional Ethics in a Pluralistic Society*, 79.

29. Camenisch, *Grounding Professional Ethics in a Pluralistic Society*, 91.

30. Mike Martin, *Meaningful Work: Rethinking Professional Ethics* (New York: Oxford University Press, 2000), 3–4.

31. Martin, *Meaningful Work*, 4.

32. Martin, *Meaningful Work*, 203.

33. William C. Bagley, "Training Public School Teachers," *Religious Education* 5 (1911): 612–40; E. Nielsen Jones, Kevin Ryan, and Karen Bohlin, *Teachers as Educators of Character: Are the Nation's Schools of Education Coming Up Short?* (Washington, DC: Character Education Partnership, 1999). D. Wakefield, *Pre-Service Teacher Training in Methods of Moral Education Instruction in United States Denominational, Private And State Teacher Education Programs* (unpublished

doctoral dissertation, Baylor University, 1996); Perry L. Glanzer and Todd Ream, "Has Teacher Education Missed Out on the 'Ethics Boom?' A Comparative Study of Ethics Requirements and Courses in Professional Majors of Christian Colleges and Universities," *Christian Higher Education* 6 (July 2007): 271–88.

34. Bok, *Our Underachieving Colleges*.

Chapter 6

How Contemporary
Student Affairs Diminishes
Moral Education

Now that the axes have done their work, when everything which was sown
has sprouted anew, we can see that the young and presumptuous people
who thought they would make our country just and happy through terror,
bloody rebellion, and civil war were themselves misled. No thanks, fathers
of education!

—Aleksandr Solzhenitsyn[1]

With the diminishment of broader forms of identity excellence in the curricular dimension of American higher education in the twentieth century,
educational administrators increasingly hired cocurricular leaders to oversee
this domain.[2] Thus, throughout the twentieth century, student affairs became
one of the fastest growing areas of the university.

Although contemporary student affairs textbooks do address moral development (in fact they have whole chapters on the subject), they tend to cover
only four theories cultivated by developmental psychologists in the 1970s and
1980s.[3] Unfortunately, morally speaking, the contemporary field of student
affairs is behind the times. In the past four decades, quite a bit has changed in
the field of moral education. To put it bluntly, this means the field of student
affairs is at least four decades behind the times. In fact, three major moral
education advances have occurred during this time that often go unmentioned
or unutilized by the student affairs profession.

This chapter examines these three developments and highlights their
importance for moral education at the collegiate level as well as the lack of
attention given to these developments by student affairs. Subsequently, the
chapter concludes by arguing such developments will be ineffective if not

97

combined with a more sophisticated understanding of identity excellence that accounts for the complex nature of moral development, moral identity and moral identity development, and other key moral components of identity excellence (discussed in part III).

THE REVIVAL OF VIRTUE ETHICS

Spurred by the publication of Alasdair MacIntyre's *After Virtue* in 1981, virtue theory and a focus on character reemerged in a host of disciplines such as philosophy, psychology, religion, K–12 education, and more. Philosophically and religiously, this approach has a long history (e.g., Aristotle, Augustine, Aquinas), but it suffered a period of academic neglect for the century before the 1980s.[4] Today, however, as the recent *Cambridge Companion to Virtue Ethics* claims, "Virtue ethics has emerged from a rich history to become one of the fastest growing fields in contemporary ethics."[5] Arguments about what virtue is, and how it is shaped or formed, exists in all the disciplines just noted.

The Example of Positive Psychology

For the sake of space, developments in each discipline are not explored herein; instead, discussion primarily focuses on the favorite academic source for the student affairs field—the discipline of psychology. Although psychologists had started to focus once again upon issues of character with the revival of virtue ethics in other fields in the 1980s and 1990s, the movement gained immense traction with the development of the field of positive psychology.

According to one telling, this movement originated around 1999 when Martin E. P. Seligman organized a group of scholars into a network that focused on the subject of what promotes human flourishing instead of focusing exclusively on the range of human dysfunctions found in the *Diagnostic and Statistical Manual of Mental Disorders* (DSM).[6] In 2004, Christopher Peterson and Martin Seligman published their positive alternative to the DSM, *Character Strengths and Virtues: A Handbook and Classification.*

Their book set forth ten criteria by which to identify character strengths before identifying six general classifications of character qualities (wisdom and knowledge, courage, humanity, justice, temperance, and transcendence). Within these categories they also placed other virtues or character qualities. They hoped that their classification could be used for "the deliberate creation of institutions that enable good character."[7]

The positive psychology movement emerged, in part, because of increased emphasis on moral pluralism and individuals being their own self-authors.

These increases created a pressing need for general guidance regarding the good life that was empirically grounded. The increasing secularization and pluralism of Western societies also meant that broad guidance could not be religious if it hoped to appeal to a wide audience. In certain Western liberal democracies, this meant a basic, common vision of the good life could no longer be assumed without individuals articulating, through social scientific means, what it might be.

Part of the attraction to the new virtue theory, particularly as expressed through positive psychology, was its indirect approach to moral formation. The new positive psychology avoided the metaphysical appeals associated with religion. For example, Judaism or Christianity often reasons in this way: *because God is this kind of being and acted in history in this manner, and you are made in God's image, therefore, you should become this kind of person in order to flourish.*

In contrast, new positive psychology starts by defining a particular virtue, operationalizing how to study it, finding correlations with other positive or negative elements that are commonly understood as related to human flourishing, and then providing wisdom about how to obtain the virtue using this kind of reasoning: *if you want to become generous, grateful, forgiving, patient, etc. you should think about, desire, and practice these things.* It promises self-chosen goodness without having to commit to a conception of human excellence informed and guided by a metanarrative or a metai-dentity. Students can be moral self-authors of virtues with little reference to the moral traditions and theories developed collectively by humans over thousands of years.

Although it tries to avoid metaphysics, this new approach to virtue does indicate limits to self-authoring. It allows for autonomy while recognizing that one cannot simply self-author a virtue in whatever way one wants. There are empirical realities regarding the human condition with which one must contend. Thus, to acquire grit, self-control, patience, or generosity—to name a few—one must learn to think certain ways, desire certain things, and engage in certain kinds of practices. In this respect, it acknowledges that like playing sports or a musical instrument, excellence in a particular area of life requires submitting to a particular moral tradition.

The other appeal of positive psychology within an ideologically pluralistic context is that people with diverse identities and moral traditions associated with those traditions can often agree upon a thin version of the virtues. For instance, in K–6 settings, parents may be asked to come to a meeting and achieve consensus, or take a vote, on what virtues they want their children taught.[8] Even politically, some degree of moral agreement can be reached with this method, although the range of moral virtues prized is also quite diverse.[9]

Ignored by Universities and Student Affairs

Most universities, by their very nature, encourage some of the virtues promoted in positive psychology and virtue theory in general, such as wisdom
and knowledge: creativity (originality, ingenuity), curiosity (interest, novelty-
seeking, openness to experience), open-mindedness (judgment, critical thinking), and love of learning and perspective (wisdom).[10] Educational leaders
seek to demonstrate and encourage virtues listed under other categories such
as integrity (e.g., honor code), gratitude (especially encouraged by alumni
associations), and fairness (e.g., social justice).

The reality, however, is that most of these are encouraged in the context
of one's identity as a professional (e.g., this is what an excellent biologist
does) and not in other areas of life. Although positive psychology has made a
significant impact on the character education movement in K–12 education—
both at the practical level and the political level—by and large, pluralistic
universities have not drawn upon positive psychology or other philosophical
or religious approaches to virtue to enhance their moral education.[11]

Though, the few authors who have tried are worth noting. Two decades
ago, a major national study pointed out that a focus on virtue is one of three
strands that can be an emphasized when it comes to moral development on
campus.[12] They argued that higher education can and should focus on incul-
cating virtues in general and, specifically, the virtues of service to the community and social justice.

Yet one still cannot find the topic of virtue in the *Journal of College
Student Development* or the *Journal of College Student Affairs* (apart from
one article). The *Journal of College and Character* is the only place where
this discussion is occurring. There is also minimal, if any, mention of virtue
or character development in references to student affairs textbooks or professional standards. Moreover, there are no references to positive psychology (an
entire field). And this is despite its emergence as one of the major academic
developments related to moral development in the field of psychology (a
favorite of student affairs).

In fact, the student affairs profession—and colleges and universities as a
whole—have been reticent to talk once again about helping students form
character or acquire virtue beyond the two citizen-oriented virtues of social
justice and service. For example, one will not find any mention of "virtue"
or "character" in the student affairs professional document explaining professional competencies.

Interestingly, the major "service" emphasized in the document is the "service to the profession and student affairs professional organizations," which
is in the interest of the professionals composing the document.[13] The primary
two virtues that professionals are both to embody and teach as professional

competencies are "social justice and inclusion." Although these virtues are certainly important, they are left alone.

In order for broad-based and effective virtue education to occur, two things are needed. Unfortunately, most of American higher education currently lacks both. First, as mentioned in the introduction, in order to cross the is-ought gap and identify virtues that are important for flourishing, one must have a clear, thick conception of human flourishing.

Since the vast majority of higher education does not—and arguably cannot—promote such a conception, the focus remains on being excellent in narrow identity fragments. Most often, this means understanding excellence in terms of being a good student, professional, or citizen. Higher education could take a second approach by seeking to educate students in a wide variety of forms of identity excellence, but it does not.

A higher education study by Schreiner and her colleagues on student thriving illustrates the limitations of the former approach. Schreiner and her colleagues explored what causes students to thrive in college transitions.[14] They defined "thriving," operationalized a study of it, found correlations with other positive or negative elements that are commonly understood as related to student flourishing, and then provided wisdom about how to promote thriving on college campuses. However, the virtue, as they defined it, is limited to the context of being a college student.

Based on their conceptualization of thriving (which includes psychological, interpersonal, and academic thriving), it would make no sense to use their research to describe how an employee or spouse could thrive. This is because employees and spouses are not measured by things like "academic determination" or "engaged learning."

In this way, this form of "thriving" is the thriving of students, and not a concept applicable to a variety of identities. Moving beyond the mere encouragement of character qualities outside of certain identity contexts would require either: 1) a commitment to a broader range of formation in different identities or 2) a compelling vision of human well-being. Currently, most of higher education has neither. There are two consequences of this current deficit.

First, faculty no longer have an interest in developing virtue in the variety of identity spheres inherently present in life. Instead, they largely focus upon what it means to be good or virtuous in one's professional life. In doing so, they have left the rest of students' moral lives to student affairs. Yet the student affairs profession appears primarily concerned with the political virtue of social justice (which is certainly needed). Yet students are not merely political animals. In its neglect of a wider understanding of virtue theory, the student affairs profession has lost and betrayed its earlier commitment to the whole person.

Second, virtue education typically finds its home in more comprehensive moral communities that do have some other common identity aside from being a good professional. Examples of such communities include faith-based groups, the military, or American Indian campus settings. Colby et al. specifically cited the United States Air Force Academy, an American Indian college named Turtle Mountain Community College, and Messiah College (now University) as examples of this approach.

Similarly, a book published by the John Templeton Foundation, *Colleges that Encourage Character Development*, recognized only nine public institutions out of one hundred colleges and universities as having demonstrated "a strong campus-wide ethos that articulates the expectation of personal and civic responsibility in all dimensions of college life."[15] Three of those institutions were military academies focusing on forming excellent military officers. Five of the other institutions did not focus upon virtue development beyond service and academic honesty. Interestingly, the only attempt to implement a character-or virtue-focused approach on a state campus at Colorado State University was short-lived.[16]

In contrast, seventy of the institutions making up Templeton's list were religiously affiliated, and most focused upon the development of a wide range of virtues. Thus, it is no surprise that one philosopher concludes regarding virtue ethics, "Thus, while no one would deny that certain character traits should be regarded as desirable around the globe, when we come to draw up a list there are difficulties as soon as we go beyond a minimalist point of view."[17]

As James Davison Hunter points out in his book *The Death of Character*, broader forms of virtue development require participation in a community with a comprehensive understanding of human flourishing and thus a comprehensive moral culture.[18] Like America itself, most of American higher education cannot provide such a culture apart from allowing smaller voluntary cultures with comprehensive visions of human flourishing and moral cultures to exist and thrive in various student groups.

Moral Identity Is Also Missing

In addition to virtue, moral identity—the key concept discussed in chapter 2—is also missing from the student affairs field. Conducting a search of the *Journal of College Student Development* or the recent textbooks for student affairs professionals yields no mention of the topic. This omission is quite surprising, since the whole domain of identity development has been a key component of student affairs study.[19] The higher education research community has ignored it as well.

The general lack of research in these areas is demonstrated in the most recent volume of *How College Affects Students*, in which a whole chapter is devoted to moral development.[20] The authors note that most scholars conceptualize moral development as a process of moving from less sophisticated to more complex moral thinking. Not surprisingly then, the college impact literature does not focus on moral identity (a different kind of moral process involving more than simply cognitive development) or virtue (which deals more with behavior). In fact, in the whole volume, there is not one mention of "moral identity" or "virtue."

The authors go on to note that "the preponderance of evidence from the 2000s emerged from scholars who adopted Kohlbergian and neo-Kohlbergian frames for understanding moral reasoning development and its relationship to college-going . . . the Kohlbergian and neo-Kohlbergian understandings of morality and its subsequent measurement dominate the research landscape with regard to college and its impact on students."[21] Later, they again point out, "Most of the research reviewed for this volume examined moral reasoning development and its relationship to participation in higher education."[22] So, if higher education student affairs does not focus upon teaching virtue in various identities, what does it do morally?

THE PRIMARY EMPHASIS UPON MORAL AUTONOMY AND SELF-AUTHORSHIP IN STUDENT AFFAIRS

Throughout the first part of the history of American higher education, a moral philosophy course was considered the capstone of the curriculum; however, by the beginning of the twentieth century, it had disappeared from the curriculum and faculty had begun transferring the responsibility of moral formation to the emerging field of student affairs.[23] As the field of student affairs grew throughout the twentieth century, it shifted from moral socialization to drawing upon sophisticated forms of moral education emerging out of the field of psychology.

As mentioned earlier, the standard texts on student development theory contain entire chapters devoted to moral development. Interestingly, in all these chapters, the authors cover four major theories from the 1970s and 1980s that student affairs administrators are expected to know and apply. The two most prominent theorists, Perry and Kohlberg, both emphasized that the ultimate end of moral development involved the need for an individual to make cognitive choices without being unduly influenced by other authorities or social groups. Kohlberg's approach, in particular, has guided most of the research regarding moral development.

Standard student development theory texts also draw upon the work of a more recent theorist, Marcia Baxter Magolda, who indirectly addresses moral development within her theory of self-authorship.[24] Based on longitudinal interviews with eighty young adults starting in college, the theory of "self-authorship" identifies the process of how students can *and* should proceed in their moral development. According to this theory, self-authorship is understood as the "capacity to internally define a *coherent* belief system and identity that coordinates mutual relations with others."[25]

Her theory also sets up a contrast between external authorities (persons, institutions, or abstract formulas) and one's internal voice. Though, interestingly, this internal voice is not the conscience. This theory, more than Perry's or Kohlberg's, stresses the role of working with others in the authoring process, but it still builds upon the need for self-authorship. Overall, a combined reading of Perry, Kohlberg, and Baxter Magolda highlights the inculcation of American individualism and the importance of autonomy.[26] Interestingly, one recent study found 28 percent of Americans now live alone (up 15 percent from 1960).[27] Viva autonomy.

The Missing Feature of Moral Mentorship in College

Thus, besides missing any focus on virtue or moral identity development, student affairs also misses something advocated by a writer often read by student affairs administrators, Sharon Daloz Parks.[28] Like earlier moral educators, Parks first turned to developmental psychology for guidance. Based upon these theorists, she claimed late adolescent moral development involved a journey from inherited forms of meaning-making espoused by authorities to a wilderness of relativism and then finally arriving at the Promised Land, which involves a "committed, inner-dependent mode of composing meaning, affirmed by a self-selected class or group."[29]

The ultimate goal of this process is students "self-conscious responsibility for [their] . . . knowing, becoming, and moral action."[30] Although young adults in Parks's theory have discovered some sense of self, they are still seeking a fit within the adult world. During this transition, Parks argued young adults need mentors, or coaches, and self-chosen, ideologically-oriented communities to guide them along this journey.

Parks defined mentors as those "who are appropriately depended upon for authoritative guidance at the time of the development of critical thought."[31] In this regard Parks departed from Perry, who at times placed an inordinate emphasis on students making their journey alone. At the time, Perry ever interpreted students' seeking of help from adults as signs of retreat from development. Instead, Parks fleshed out the type of mentor necessary for guiding students in these processes. She noted, "The good mentor simply recognizes that the young adult is still dependent in substantial ways upon authority outside the self, while at the same time, the mentor is a champion of the competence and potential the young life represents."[32]

Applying her theory to the university setting, Parks also departed from other popular theories. She suggested the role of the university is to provide direct mentors and mentoring communities that assist young people in this process. Instead of buying into the modern ideal that separates the objective from the subjective, facts from values, Parks maintained that higher education does and should serve "the young adult as his or her primary community of imagination, within which every professor is potentially a spiritual guide and every syllabus a confession of faith."[33]

According to Parks, "The mentoring professor, therefore, must convene and mediate among multiple perspectives, composing a trustworthy community of imagination—a community of confirmation and contradiction."[34] Overall, Parks placed much more emphasis upon the role of guiding experts and the importance of communities than earlier developmental theorists. She also does not assume that a sharp discontinuity with older moral mentors or models is good.

The limits of Parks's proposal lie less in her recommendations than in what she leaves out. Who are or should be the moral mentors? Those who are the best moral mentors (i.e., coaches, as previous chapters identify them) and moral models, similar to those who are experts or mentors in any field, are those who demonstrate and/or can teach expertise in building a whole, moral life. Models and mentors are experts in living out a particular vision of the good life within a particular community with particular ways of thinking within various spheres of life. How do students identify these models and mentors within the various traditions, resources, and moral assets that they bring with them to their undergraduate experiences?

Interestingly, there is little discussion in the literature about the role of student affairs professionals, the ones now largely in charge of identity excellence in areas other than professional excellence, regarding moral mentoring. Few student affairs leaders have taken up Parks's admonition that during the collegiate stage of moral and faith development, students need mentors.[35] In fact, neither Parks's work nor mentoring are mentioned in the indexes of the most prominent student affairs texts.[36] Instead, the dominant theory taught in student affairs texts focuses upon the importance of student self-authorship.

The Core Problem: Two Understandings of Moral Expertise

At the heart of this debate are two different understandings of moral expertise. A 1975 issue of the *Journal of Moral Education* discussing moral expertise illustrates the tension. According to one group of authors, developing moral expertise involves becoming an autonomous moral reasoner and chooser.[37] In contrast, another author proclaimed, "Morality is not simply a matter of skill in moral reasoning and judgment. Character, conduct, and consequences are also important and, in some ways, more basic."[38] Unfortunately, within student affairs over the past half century, the former authors' views have carried the day.

This book argues that student affairs need to help students develop the second form of moral expertise. Yet, when moral formation is viewed as the development of expertise for living the good life, two problems for student affairs arise. First, when a student—be they athlete, musician, or artist—come to the university, university mentors and coaches have often recruited those students for their current expertise and then build upon this past education.

Yet as they maintain approaches to moral expertise focusing solely on moral autonomy, student affairs leaders often view previous comprehensive moral communities and educators as problematic authorities. Thus, a well-known higher education theorist, Vincent Tinto, claimed, "In order to become fully incorporated in the life of the college, individuals have to physically as well as socially dissociate themselves from the communities of the past."[39] This disassociation involved the moral domain, since,

> Such communities differ from college not only in composition but also in the values, norms, and behavioral and intellectual styles that characterize their everyday life. As a result, the process leading to the adoption of behaviors and norms appropriate to the life of the college necessarily requires some degree of transformation and perhaps rejection of the norms of past communities.[40]

However, if moral expertise shares important communal and framework elements (i.e., a coherent community with a clear telos and performance metrics constrained by rules and reached by virtues acquired through deliberate practice), then these communities and mentors are vital building blocks as students progress toward moral expertise.

Developing moral expertise requires mentoring and coaching. The best professionals in their fields still have these figures in their lives, even at the highest level of accomplishment. Certainly, individuals are still the primary authors of their own performance in these cases, and we do, in fact, teach people to reevaluate (though not to dismiss entirely) their prior education, identities, beliefs, and behaviors from a critical perspective. Yet even accomplished people need significant forms of mentorship from top-level experts. These experts are not simply random authorities; they are professionals who have mastered the profession themselves, or at least the coaching of it.

Moral expertise also requires a coherent moral community of character focused upon a clear human identity with clear ends and a performance metrics. Furthermore, moral formation requires coauthorship in relationship with moral mentors and models who guide deliberate practice and offer wisdom. Or, to use an academic analogy, individuals are the primary authors, but they rely upon coauthors for wisdom. The democratic deficit model fails to adequately address this empirical reality, especially the importance of identity-based moral communities and mentors.

In the end, emphasizing self-authorship as a *normative* outlook not only contradicts how we develop expertise in other identity domains, but it also contradicts particular moral traditions of identity excellence. Like the professions, these traditions of thought look to moral mentors, coaches, or guides—as well as moral models—as key elements of developing moral expertise. According to these moral traditions, an extreme form of self-authorship without reliance upon moral experts actually leads to the vice of pride.

CONCLUSION

Amazingly, it appears that student affairs and higher education researchers have missed out almost completely on three of the burgeoning intellectual movements of the past three and a half decades with regard to moral development. It is time for the field to move beyond a fixation upon cognitive moral development and reasoning, discovering more recent research and approaches that address the whole moral person. Educators can do more to teach students about virtue, the key components of identity excellence, a moral vision for human flourishing, and the elements of a comprehensive moral culture.

NOTES

1. Aleksandr Solzhenitsyn, *Essays on Civil Disobedience*, ed. Bob Blaisdell (Mineola, NY: Dover Publications, 2016), 158.

2. Julie Reuben, *The Making of the Modern University: Intellectual Transformation and the Marginalization of Morality* (Chicago: University of Chicago Press, 1996).

3. Wendy K. Killam and Suzanne Degges-White, *College Student Development: Applying Theory to Practice on the Diverse* Campus (New York: Springer Publishing Company, 2017); Lori D. Patton, Kristen A. Renn, Florence Guido-DiBrito, and Stephen John Quaye, *Student Development in College: Theory, Research, and Practice*, 3rd ed. (San Francisco: Jossey-Bass & Pfeiffer, 2016).

4. For an essay proposing some reasons for this neglect see Dorothea Frede, "The Historical Decline of Virtue Ethics," in *The Cambridge Companion to Virtue Ethics*, ed. Daniel C. Russell (New York: Cambridge University Press, 2013), 124–48.

5. Russell, *The Cambridge Companion to Virtue Ethics,* i.

6. Ed Diener, "Positive Psychology: Past, Present, and Future," *Oxford Handbook of Positive Psychology* 2nd ed., eds. C. R. Snyder and Shane J. Lopez (New York: Oxford University Press, 2009), 8.

7. Christopher Peterson and Martin Seligman, *Character Strengths and Virtues: A Handbook and Classification* (Oxford and New York: Oxford University Press, 2004), 5.

8. Thomas Lickona, *Educating for Character: How Our Schools Can Teach Respect and Responsibility* (New York: Bantam, 1991).

9. Perry Glanzer and Andrew Milson, "Legislating the Good: A Survey and Evaluation of Contemporary Character Education Evaluation," *Educational Policy* 20, 3 (2006): 525–50.

10. For a philosophical perspective on the intellectual virtues see Jason S. Baehr, *The Inquiring Mind on Intellectual Virtues and Virtue Epistemology* (New York: Oxford University Press, 2011) and Jason S. Baehr, *Intellectual Virtues and Education: Essays in Applied Virtue Epistemology* (New York: Routledge, Taylor & Francis Group, 2016).

11. For an example of the political influence see Glanzer and Andrew, "Legislating the Good."

12. Anne Colby, Thomas Ehrlich, Elizabeth Beaumont, and Jason Stephens, *Educating Citizens: Preparing America's Undergraduates for Lives of Moral Responsibility* (San Francisco: Jossey-Bass, 2003).

13. ACPA and NASPA, *Professional Competency Areas for Student Affairs Practitioners* (Washington, DC: ACPA and NASPA, 2015), 19.

14. Laurie A. Schreiner, Michelle C. Louis, and Denise D. Nelson, *Thriving in Transitions: A Research-Based Approach to College Student Success*, 2nd ed. (Columbia: National Resource Center for the First-Year Experience & Students in Transition, University of South Carolina, 2020).

15. John Templeton Foundation, ed., *Colleges that Encourage Character Development* (Radnor, PA: Templeton Foundation Press, 1999), v.

16. For example, see Perry L. Glanzer and Todd C. Ream, *Christianity and Moral Identity in Higher Education* (New York: Palgrave Macmillan, 2009), chapters 5 and 6.

17. Frede, "The Historical Decline of Virtue Ethics," 144.

18. James Davison Hunter, *The Death of Character: Moral Education in an Age Without Good or Evil* (New York: Basic Books, 2008).

19. See Arthur Chickering and Linda Reisser, *Education and Identity* (San Francisco: Jossey-Bass, 1996).

20. Matthew J. Mayhew, Ernest T. Pascarella, and Patrick T. Terenzini (2016), *How College Affects Students. Volume 3, 21st Century Evidence That Higher Education Works* (San Francisco, CA: Jossey-Bass, 2016).

21. Mayhew et al., *How College Affects Students*, 332.

22. Mayhew et al., *How College Affects Students*, 336.

23. Julie Reuben, *The Making of the Modern University: Intellectual Transformation and the Marginalization of Morality* (Chicago: University of Chicago Press, 1996); Douglas Sloan, "The Teaching of Ethics in the American Undergraduate

Curriculum, 1876–1976," in *Ethics Teaching in Higher Education*, eds. Daniel Callahan and Sissela Bok (New York: Plenum Press, 1980).

24. Marcia B. Baxter Magolda, *Making Their Own Way: Narratives for Transforming Higher Education to Promote Self-Development* (Sterling, VA: Stylus Press, 2001); Marcia B. Baxter Magolda, *Creating Contexts for Learning and Self-Authorship: Constructive-Developmental Pedagogy* (Nashville, TN: Vanderbilt University Press, 1999); Marcia B. Baxter Magolda and Patricia M. King, *Theories and Models of Practice to Educate for Self-Authorship* (Sterling, VA: Stylus, 2004).

25. Magolda and King, *Theories and Models of Practice to Educate for Self-Authorship*, 8.

26. For more on this point see Perry L. Glanzer, *The Dismantling of Moral Education: How Higher Education Reduced the Human Identity* (Lanham, MD: Rowman & Littlefield, 2022).

27. Mark Mather et al., "What the 2020 Census Will Tell Us About a Changing America," *Population Bulletin* 74, no. 1 (Washington, DC: Population Reference Bureau, 2019), 13.

28. Sharon Daloz Parks, *Big Questions, Worthy Dreams: Mentoring Emerging Adults in Their Search for Meaning, Purpose, and Faith*, rev. ed. (San Francisco: Jossey-Bass, 2011).

29. Parks, *Big Questions, Worthy Dreams*, 70.

30. Parks, *Big Questions, Worthy Dreams*, 77.

31. Parks, *Big Questions, Worthy Dreams*, 128.

32. Parks, *Big Questions, Worthy Dreams*, 129.

33. Parks, *Big Questions, Worthy Dreams*, 134.

34. Parks, *Big Questions, Worthy Dreams*, 168.

35. Parks, *Big Questions, Worthy Dreams*.

36. Killam and Degges-White, *College Student Development*; Patton et al., *Student Development in College: Theory.*

37. John Woods and Douglas Walton, "Moral Expertise," *Journal of Moral Education* 5, no. 1 (1975), 13–18.

38. Peter Miller, "Who Are the Moral Experts? *Journal of Moral Education* 5, no. 1 (1975): 4.

39. Vincent Tinto, *Leaving College: Rethinking the Causes and Cures of Student Attrition*, 2nd ed. (Chicago: University of Chicago Press, 1993), 96.

40. Tinto, *Leaving College.*

PART III

The Pursuit of Human Flourishing through Identity Excellence

Education shall be directed to the full development of the human personality and to the strengthening of respect for human rights and fundamental freedoms.

—United Nations Declaration of Human Rights (1948)[1]

One of the primary arguments of this book is that whereas American higher education used to be about acquiring wisdom from mentors in multiple areas of human identity, it now largely focuses on moral learning in two identity areas: our professional and citizenship identities. The diminishment of moral education to these two identities not only undermines our attempts to engage in more human and holistic approaches to moral education, but it also undermines our efforts to achieve a more human professional life and social justice in our civic life. The result is that higher education creates narrowly focused moral absolutists focused on issues of citizenship.[2]

To educate students regarding moral expertise, higher education needs an approach to moral and general education that understands that professional or political identities and stories cannot be the ultimate source of meaning and purpose, virtue, practices, and wisdom that guide the rest of our lives. Indeed, creating self-authors who glory in personal autonomy, individual expressivism, and narrow forms of citizenship excellence supported by Meta-Democracy is not the ultimate identity, end, and story for most Americans.

What might a different form of moral education look like—one that takes seriously our various identities, the moral traditions associated with them, and the conflicts that occur between them? The answer to the danger of socializing young people is not to stop socializing them in favor of just presenting them challenging and ahistorical moral dilemmas (à la Kohlberg). No, the answer is found in providing educational socialization consistent with a respect for individual and communal rights.[3]

Such an education recognizes that young students need to be introduced to traditions of identity excellence. After all, if individuals and communities are to make moral choices, they must know what their choices are. To put it another way, knowing how to act requires one to know the moral plays or narratives that they might be able to inhabit. As Warren Nord puts it:

> What is essential is that [students] understand (and feel) the deep justifications of contemporary moral ideas and ideals. . . . The great virtue of a liberal arts education is that it situates students in thick moral, civic, and religious traditions—traditions that make sense of our moral values and provide deep justifications for them (and give students ground on which to stand in confronting the materialism and often mindless individualism of popular culture and the relativism of so much of our intellectual life). It provides the roots of morality.[4]

This kind of liberal arts education in moral traditions requires two forms of educational justice.

First, a liberal democracy must allow—as America currently does at all levels of education—multiple forms of educational communities from which parents and then college students can choose. Some of these educational communities are publicly funded and others privately funded. Second, within publicly funded educational institutions, younger students must be socialized according to commonly agreed upon elements of moral identity excellence. Meanwhile, older students must receive a liberal arts education covering the range of moral traditions active in American life.

In other words, the need to educate students morally remains pressing. However, meeting the need requires systems of moral education that acknowledge and incorporate the following: respect for the human will, the need for identity development, individual motivation, and regard for pluralism. Part of the job of higher education is to educate students about all these elements in light of larger questions about what it means to be a good neighbor, American, child, spouse, friend, caretaker of the environment, steward of culture, and more. Higher education should be providing a liberal education about various traditions of moral thought and identity excellence.

The chapters in part III set forth a vision of education in the Great Identities. What makes an identity great? First, the Great Identities are those most commonly employed in forming a moral identity. The identities themselves may be inherited or chosen, but individuals choose to pursue excellence within each identity to enhance an understanding of the good life. Of course, some of these identities will vary from person to person. Each person will be forced by reality to make choices about how to be excellent in their various identities.

In addition to indicating the importance of these identities, the term "great" is also used in a second, moral sense. Great Identities are the ones in which humans seek excellence most of their lives. Thus, these identities are often the ones by which people determine whether or not someone has lived a good life.[5] For instance, someone may rightly be deemed an excellent physicist. However, the same person may not be deemed an excellent human being, particularly if they failed in multiple marriages, neglected to parent their children in any significant way, abused the environment, and died from health complications related to their own unhealthy choices. Empirically speaking, the Great Identities are a key part of any major vision for the good life.[6]

Third, these identities are also great in that humanity has had perennial conversations throughout history about what it means to be excellent in each of these identities. Society has continually talked—and even argued—about what makes a good mother, bodily steward, steward of money, neighbor, and more. Granted, there is also some important agreement on the moral elements associated with these identities as well (e.g., "Like a good neighbor, State Farm is there"). Still, history is no stranger to arguments concerning what it means to be excellent in these identities. In other words, the Great Identities are bound together by the historical persistence of these identity categories across cultures along with an innate human need to figure out what it means to be good within these identities.

To be clear, not all aspects of these human identities should be equated in how they are derived, socially constructed, or chosen. After all, there are significant differences among these identities. The identity categories used in a particular cultural context are not always ontologically inevitable or immutable. For example, those with mixed racial heritage often socially construct and prioritize a particular racial identity using categories of race specific to a country's historical context. Still, while there is some choice regarding identities, there are limits to the array of identities an individual can choose or reaffirm.

On a related aside, some of these identities remain important in particular countries in so far as they are related to "identity politics." Unfortunately, such discussions most often center on what it means for particular marginalized identity groups to be excellent citizens. In other words, those discussions are primarily dealing with political power or at best pertain to social justice. These conversations are vitally important. After all, those who have been politically abused, targeted for genocide, systematically discriminated against, or randomly persecuted throughout their lives due to a particular identity they hold should work passionately to correct that social injustice! (And, so should others.) Even so, obtaining political forms of social justice or being an excellent citizen should not be confused with being excellent in other identities.

Oddly, although figuring out what it means to be excellent in the Great Identities is likely the most important thing we will do in life, higher education tends to focus on only two of these identities: our vocational and political identities. Some institutions also have gender or racial studies departments, but these entities often only address one or two more of the Great Identities (at best) for a few students. We need to give all the Great Identities more academic attention.

NOTES

1. The Universal Declaration of Human Rights (1948), article 26 (3). Retrieved August 9, 2020 from http://www.un.org/en/documents/udhr/index.html.

2. Miloš Broćić and Andrew Miles, "College and the 'Culture War': Assessing Higher Education's Influence on Moral Attitudes," *American Sociological Review*, September 2021, doi:10.1177/00031224211041094.

3. Warren Nord, *Does God Make a Difference? Taking Religion Seriously in Our Schools and Universities* (New York: Oxford, 2011), 264–83.

4. Nord, *Does God Make a Difference?*, 268.

5. Perry L. Glanzer, Theodore F. Cockle, Sarah Schnitker, and Jonathan Hill, "American College Students' Understandings of the Good Life: A Grounded Theory," unpublished manuscript currently under review.

6. Perry L. Glanzer, Jonathan P. Hill, and Jessica A. Robinson, "Emerging Adults' Conceptions of Purpose and the Good Life: A Classification and Comparison," *Youth & Society* 50, 6 (2018): 715–33.

Chapter 7

Teaching Excellence in the Great Identities

A Revised Educational Frame

This chapter does one of the most idiotic things you can do in higher education—it makes a case for changing general education. Despite the fact that even the smallest of curricular changes to general education takes an act of God, the argument in this book leads to one logical conclusion—we need to reform the whole system. Realistically, this means abolishing general education as it currently exists in most institutions. We need a revolution, and we need to take general education to the guillotine. Revolutions and guillotines are evocative (provocative, even!) images, but the reality is that subtle changes over time only serve to dress up a failed concept when a systemic solution is necessary.

What exactly might an educational revolution entail? John Dewey similarly suggested a revolution when he claimed that education should revolve around the student:

The old education . . . may be summed up by stating that the center of gravity is outside the child. It is in the teacher, the textbook, anywhere and everywhere you please except in the immediate instincts and activities of the child himself. . . . Now the change which is coming into our education is the shifting of the center of gravity. It is a change, a revolution, not unlike that introduced by Copernicus when the astronomical center shifted from the earth to the sun. In this case the child becomes the sun about which the appliances of education revolve; he is the center about which they are organized.[2]

The best pedagogy and curriculum always start with a key question about what is most *relevant* to the student.[3]

In the case of general education, the relevant question is: Who am I? When students move into a residence hall, they hopefully realize they are suddenly tasked with being a good neighbor. They will continue to learn what it means to be a good student, a good friend, and a good romantic friend. Many are learning to steward their things, their body, their race, and the environment in new ways. They must learn anew what it means to be a son or daughter, a good religious or nonreligious person, and a citizen. They must learn what it means to be excellent in the Great Identities.

General education must be reimagined to focus on the Great Identities. The agreements these identities provide about general human functions help overcome the fragmentation of human identity common within moral education. In other words, essential elements of human identity still exist by which everyone can learn to understand and pursue excellence. In fact, understanding the good life as a whole requires thinking through what it means to be good within these foundational identities.

THE KEY MORAL ARGUMENT

The primary argument for teaching the Great Identities in general education is that it focuses upon whom the university should serve—the student. The current system of majors serves the discipline or profession associated with a particular major, but general education should focus on whom the university is ultimately meant to serve.[4] As John Dewey noted, changing the focus from the teacher and the curriculum to the student involves a revolutionary curricular transformation.[5]

Although focusing on students and their Great Identities may seem to foster a preoccupation with one's self, in reality, it does what any good teacher should do. It starts with students' interests and identities and then moves outward to the moral obligations and challenges of these identities to the wider world in three particular ways.

First, when understood as focusing upon not only a particular human identity, but also upon what it means to be excellent in that identity, the conversation centers on excellence instead of politics. Being an excellent friend is not simply a concern about who has the most power in the friendship, although that is a component. Instead, consideration focuses on the purpose of friendship; the rules and practices of friendship; the virtues associated with friendship—love, care, forgiveness, and generosity; how one practices for friendship; and more. Students want and need to have moral conversations about what it means to be good or excellent in areas of their identity with which they will be wrestling the rest of their lives.

Moreover, unlike an English composition class focused on critiquing Fox News, a course at an actual university, identity conversations are timeless and undertaken by all humans globally. Everywhere in the world, humans ask about what it means to be a good neighbor, steward of resources, friend, a steward of one's body, citizen, family member, and more. Moreover, the pursuit of excellence in these elements remains pertinent to students throughout their lives and not just during a particular phase.

Second, a focus on identity excellence keeps general education from being self-centered in another way. Certainly, these courses would capture the students' attention because they are relevant, but they would also require students to situate themselves within a historical context—a vitally important skill. Knowing what it means to be excellent in any identity is impossible without encountering the past conversations about what it means to be excellent—the so-called moral tradition around the identity. Therefore, a general education focused on identity excellence would help students understand commonalities and differences throughout history regarding excellence in various identities.

By nature, the identity focus connects students with broader community identities and the larger stories and moral traditions associated with those identities, something at which higher education is currently abysmal.[6] Throughout history, humans have fostered robust conversations among different philosophical and religious traditions regarding what it means to be a good friend, a good steward of your race and ethnicity, a steward of culture, and more. Schooling needs to expose students to these intellectual conversations. In this way, a Great Identities course of study is student-centered without being self-centered.

Third and finally, many current general education courses focus on providing information. Take, for instance, one institution's required course on the US Constitution and constitutional law. Although such a course is valuable, its purveyors assume students' interest in this knowledge.

Education in the Great Identities, in contrast, maintains that discussing information in the context of the identity and moral ideals for which that information is relevant proves much more valuable and engaging. For example, rather than merely discussing information about the US Constitution, a Great Identity conversation would focus on what it means to be a good citizen, which involves knowing the Constitution and its interpretive legal *and* *moral* tradition.

Those who live in liberal democracies argue about the good life. Teaching about the Great Identities is basically introducing students to moral conversations about identity excellence. Moreover, for any of the ethical objectives in general education to be integrated into students' lives, students must acquire a moral identity associated with a particular identity. As Irene Clark, summarizing the findings from neuropsychology, observed, "Involvement in academic genres may require students to assume a particular identity when they write or participate in class, but what current brain study suggests is that this involvement is a type of 'performance' that does not necessarily result in profound identity change."[7]

Many of Clark's thoughts about helping students learn different genres and identities associated with those genres prove helpful in learning to think morally within one's various identities. She goes on:

> But the act of performing itself can also result in an increased consciousness of the performance, so that when students leave our classrooms, when they greet their friends, participate in a sport, tweet, send Instagrams, or attend a family barbecue, they will be able to shift identities, sometimes easily, sometimes with difficulty. But we can help students become aware that they are doing so, enabling them to choose who they wish to be according to situation and context.[8]

Similarly, when students are taught to think about the different moral traditions concerning what it means to be an excellent student, athlete, friend, or family member, they can then make more informed and critical moral choices about their performance in these identities. They also learn how to prioritize identities when choosing between them.

Additional Arguments

Of course, other important reasons for a new approach to general education address weaknesses with the old approach.

First, these courses are naturally interdisciplinary and would need to be taught in an interdisciplinary manner. For instance, figuring out what it means to care for the earth necessitates hearing from experts in various STEM fields. Similarly, understanding stewardship of culture requires hearing from those in various culture-creating fields, as well as an expert in personal finance. Moreover, thinking about what it means to be an excellent friend—especially a romantic friend—requires the help of philosophers, theologians, and psychologists, probably all together. Exploring excellence in any of these identities would require numerous disciplines.[9]

Second, general education too often serves the interests of the academic departments and the disciplines, who win the general education course wars, instead of students. Educating students for human excellence requires usurping academic departments, the contemporary centers of power—and vested interests—within universities.

In reality, learning about the moral discussion we have had throughout history regarding what it means to be a good citizen, a good family member, a good neighbor, a good steward of resources, a good friend, etc. involves all the disciplines. Yet we know that challenges to human flourishing are not simply sociological, historical, or psychological. Of course, students need to learn what it means to think sociologically, economically, and psychologically about all these identities, but it helps for students to learn how to employ these critical thinking tools in the context of relevant identities with which they will wrestle all their lives.

Of course, scholars find transferring knowledge from one domain to another is one of the most difficult skills to teach.[10] Learning excellence, such as the virtue of love, in one identity context (e.g., spouse) does not mean that element will easily translate into another identity context (e.g., neighbor). As was explained in chapter 3, human behavior does not exhibit what scholars call cross-situational stability—consistency when living out different identities. However, teaching identity excellence in the Great Identities requires students to understand the importance of drawing upon these academic tools or perspectives to achieve various forms of human excellence.

Second, this approach to general education is neither politically conservative (like the Great Books approach is often perceived) nor politically liberal (as emphasis on gender or race studies is often perceived). The problem with both the Western civilization and Great Books approaches to general education is that they were usually associated with a conservative political tradition (whether accurate or not).

Granted, general education focusing on the Great Identities may be seen as liberal since Progressives have dominated conversations of identity. However, Progressives have been primarily concerned with identity politics—the power associated with certain identities–as opposed to identity excellence—what it means to be a good man or woman, an excellent friend, or an excellent steward of the culture.[11] Certainly, understanding what it means to be excellent necessarily involves political considerations of power; however, classroom discussion should place primary emphasis on the moral dimension of these issues.

In short, teaching the Great Identities moves beyond an engagement in an identity or culture war for power to seeking and finding the good. In fact, an overemphasis upon power dynamics has led to a focus on politically relevant identities (e.g., citizenship, race, gender, etc.) at the exclusion of other identities (e.g., What does it mean to be a good friend, father or mother, or neighbor, steward of culture?). Yet conversations about all prove vitally important, both in the personal and public lives of all people.

Finally, and perhaps best of all, these kinds of conversations do a much better job of serving the future good life of students. Yes, students must figure out how to be a good biologist, historian, or accountant, but they also need to figure out excellence in other areas of their lives. In this respect, identity conversations relate to the felt needs of students and are quite relevant to them, which is one of the keys to effective college teaching.[12]

In fact, many of the new courses discussed in both higher education and popular newspapers are of this type. For example, some time ago *The Chronicle of Higher Education* reported about Michelle Lampl's new course, Health 100. An anthropology professor at Emory University, she had become concerned about students' health, even declaring that health of late adolescents "is a national emergency."[13]

Thus, Lampl designed a required course that, at its core, explores what it means to be an excellent steward of one's body. Or, as *The Chronicle* described it, a course that "aims to get students to make healthier choices to improve their well-being, including diet and mental health."[14] In a brilliant stroke of pedagogy, classes of less than nineteen students are taught by upperclassman who seek to make them practical. For instance, one reading is about how sleep influences health.

Similarly, *The Atlantic* wrote glowingly about a set of courses described as Marriage 101. The first lesson is, "There are no soul mates."[15] *The Chronicle* also wrote about a first-year course at the University of Virginia entitled "The Art and Science of Human Flourishing" that explores the scholarly research about what makes people thrive.[16]

In fact, the University of North Carolina at Chapel Hill and the University of Denver hold Adulting 101 workshops that help students with basic skills that are all connected to the Great Identities.[17] Students clearly desire education on stewarding one's financial resources, body, and time. Interestingly, the University of Denver website even touts, "Learn the life skills you're not learning in class."[18] This begs the question: Why are students not learning about identity excellence in their classes?

WHAT TEACHING THE GREAT
IDENTITIES MIGHT INVOLVE

The following section outlines what a general education in the Great Identities might look like. Of course, the short court descriptions will be inadequate for the subject, but they do provide insight into what this approach to general education might involve:

First Year

First-year students should learn excellence in those identities that are most relevant to a beginning student seeking to figure out some of life's basics.

Friends, Neighbors, and Enemies (First Semester)

All students will be friends, neighbors, and enemies throughout their lives. These normative, relational categories take on added significance at residential colleges where students encounter new friendships, neighbors, and enemies. Unfortunately, faculty often leave discussions of such matters solely to the cocurricular arena of college life, which tends to define student success using the categories most relevant to the institution. For the institution, "student success" means measuring campus involvement, retention, and graduation rates. They are concerned with student belonging, but only in so far as it leads to persistence of tuition-paying students.[19] Surely, success in higher education is more than just these measures.[20]

Students, for example, know that success in life involves having quality friendships (and some even define this relational goal as one of their major life purposes).[21] Furthermore, scholarship has revealed that an increasingly individualistic and autonomous culture has created a crisis of both friendship and other forms of social connection.[22] Friendships and healthy social connections, even with our enemies, require knowledge of the various ways moral traditions develop relationships, a cultivated love and affection for such connections, and practice engaging in them.

A more human general education would help students reflect upon the characteristics and normative ideals associated with these identities. Students would explore their own conceptions of these categories in light of other moral traditions' approaches to these matters. Students might read materials including Aristotle's writings on friendship, Robert Putnam's *Bowling Alone*, and Martin Luther King Jr.'s sermon on loving one's enemies. Exposure to such writings would help students realize that practical matters—often viewed as involving innate skills and knowledge—actually require serious thought, study, and deliberate practice to achieve excellence.

The Excellent Student (First Semester)

Recently, some success at reviving virtue ethics has been attained by asking questions related to the most obvious identity for students: What does it mean to be an excellent student? Or said another way, what does it mean to develop intellectual virtue?[23] Students who were excellent in high school will not automatically be excellent learners in college.

Consider the basics, such as the purpose of higher education. The vast majority of students think an excellent student is someone who obtains a credential to get a job or get into advanced professional or graduate education. Examples of common student language regarding the purpose of education include:

- I think practically it is where you become prepared for your future career.
- Well, ideally, the purpose of college is to basically further your education in hopes of furthering your career and getting a job.
- The purpose of college is to learn and prepare for your future in a given field.
- I think college is to help you succeed in life and focus on what your interest is to help you in a job field that you would succeed in.
- I think that's what most college students sign up for when they sign up for colleges and education to get a degree in a specialized field to then go into a work field to use that.
- For me, the purpose of college is getting my degree so I can go on and pursue teaching. And I'm planning on minoring in Arabic because I want to live in the Middle East. And so, this is just like the next stepping-stone for furthering my future.[24]

Obviously, from the very start, students need help to think more deeply and critically about the purpose of being a student in higher education. Doing so will require evaluating the narrative that is currently guiding their understanding of the excellent student, along with various alternative narratives and purposes.

Students also must learn about other moral elements. For example, even at the best of universities—in fact, more so at the best universities, since students with the lowest and highest grades tend to cheat the most—three-quarters of students break the most basic rules about cheating.[25] As a result, educators need to help students think deeply and critically about the basic rules governing the practice of being a student.

Finally, many students arrive without the basic intellectual virtues required for being excellent students. Jason Baehr provides a helpful catalog of such virtues in his excellent study on intellectual virtues, some of which are listed in Table 7.1.[26] Most students never really learn how to acquire these virtues in high school. Thus, many universities offer study skills courses, but these are usually offered outside of a normative context that encompasses a larger purpose.

Consequently, the course goals focus merely on instrumental academic skills or practices disconnected from connected to intellectual virtues (e.g., how to study/write better, how to manage your time, etc.). Such courses have

Table 7.1

Inquiry-Relevant Challenge	Corresponding Intellectual Virtues
Initial motivation	Inquisitiveness, reflectiveness, contemplativeness, curiosity, wonder
Sufficient and proper focusing	Attentiveness, thoroughness, sensitivity to detail, careful observation, scrutiny, perceptiveness
Consistency in evaluation	Intellectual justice, fairmindedness, consistency, objectivity, impartiality, open-mindedness
Intellectual "wholeness" or integrity	Intellectual integrity, honesty, humility, transparency, self-awareness, self-scrutiny
Mental flexibility	Imaginativeness, creativity, intellectual flexibility, open-mindedness, agility, adaptability
Endurance	Intellectual perseverance, determination, patience, courage, diligence, tenacity

now found their way into the curriculum at many colleges and universities under the guise of what we call first-year seminars. It would be helpful to imagine what a first semester course might look like that developed intellectual virtues for the sake of engaging in the life-long pursuit of wisdom.[27]

Stewardship I: Self (First Semester)

What does it mean to love oneself in a way that leads to one's own bodily flourishing? An increasing percentage of students do not experience bodily flourishing in college.[28] Institutions that have integrated courses like those at Emory University have seen positive effects, but these courses are still far from being ubiquitous.[29] Thus, this course, while drawing upon the subject matter of the disciplines of the health sciences and ethics, would examine answers related to the normative question of how one best promotes bodily flourishing.

What ends should one pursue, what virtues should one acquire, or what practices should one develop in contribution to bodily flourishing? Such questions are life-long normative questions about which students should be taught to think critically and to make practical commitments. Unless you teach someone to take care of themselves, they cannot even begin to take care of the rest of the natural or cultural world. Thus, stewardship of the natural world starts with our natural selves (i.e., we are not somehow separated from the rest of nature).

First-year students, in particular, struggle with bodily stewardship. The oft trivialized phrase "freshman fifteen" provides confirmation. Yet stewardship of one's body involves more than eating. It relates to binge drinking and sexual activity, two major issues among college students.[30] Yet colleges rarely require students to think about these issues in light of the historical moral traditions already developed for bodily flourishing.

Moreover, students are often not encouraged to think through the purpose of their activities in these areas, the narratives guiding their behavior, the rules they need to know, the virtues and practices they should develop, and the mentors and sources of wisdom they should find. When students are given the chance to think through their actions in these areas, they often gain new moral insights.[31]

Stewardship II: Race and/or Ethnicity (Second Semester)

Every human being must think about what it means to steward their race or ethnicity. Whether conceived as a gift of God, fate, or social construction (or perhaps some of all three), students must learn to steward their race and ethnicity in their lived context. Everyone has this responsibility, whether a part of a majority or minority.

Yet those races and ethnicities with the most power, and perhaps with a history of past injustices toward minorities, have the greatest need to think morally about what they must do with power and privilege. The conversation must be a moral discussion and not simply an attainment of knowledge. For example, George Yancey thinks about the moral dimension of race relationships in America as follows:

> Let me tell you a story. There was a man and a woman who were married. They were married for 15 years. But it was a horrible marriage. The husband was very abusive to his wife. His abuse was mental, physical, and even sexual. The wife withstood this horrible situation for as long as she could. At the end of those 15 years, she told him that their marriage was at an end. The husband realized how awful he had been. He decided that he would not be abusive anymore. He told his wife he would stop his pattern of abuse. And he did. So, the couple could live happily ever after.[32]

Hopefully, it is apparent how unrealistic—even problematic—this story is.

Yancey uses this parable to illuminate how whites should be careful about wanting to just forget the past and move forward in race relationships. As Yancey points out:

> The husband and the wife had built up a decade and a half of dysfunctional relationship patterns which needed to be reformed. The husband had the lion share of the work to change his ways. Not only did he have to refuse to engage in abusive behavior, but he had to learn patience and sensitivity to the needs of his wife. His years of abuse took away his rights to engage with his wife in ways that other men had. He had to go the extra mile to work towards regaining her trust. In his communication with her, he must begin to learn and appreciate the work he needed to do.

Of course, some colleagues of color may think Yancey's story is too simplistic. One could argue that it would be better to imagine a husband whose wife was forced to marry him. Moreover, that same husband had kidnapped, tortured, and even murdered many of the wife's relatives. Now, the husband wanted to establish peace with his wife and ask forgiveness. Clearly, this change alters the level of moral responsibility. Of course, a helpful class would have students read various critiques of how to understand this story given the moral responsibilities of various groups.

For example, Yancey notes that the wife has different moral responsibilities in the story:

> She had to deal with her anger in healthy ways so that it did not fester and grow poisonous in her. She learned that she could also be unfair to her husband and that communicating with him was better for the long-term health of their relationship than manipulating his feelings of guilt. Indeed, with this careful communication, she learned when her reactions were justifiably based on reasonable fears and when they were unfair emotional blackmail.[33]

Again, some may argue that Yancey overstates the responsibility of the wife, claiming that minorities rarely engage in this behavior. In other words, Yancey's story is not the only moral perspective one could take. Indeed, other moral traditions take other perspectives. Thus, the important academic goal is to help students understand these different moral traditions. Instead of merely chanting moral slogans, students must learn to think through the different moral traditions concerning how to steward race and ethnicity.

The Second Year

Religious or Secular Identity

One of the most important identities in the lives of humans around the world concerns their religious or secular identity. However, many American students educated in secular public schools do not understand that different secular and religious identities have epistemological and moral implications for learning. In fact, they may not even realize that understanding the world as secular is a relatively recent phenomenon.[34]

As Warren Nord found in his study of K–16 education in public schools, there is no overt hostility to religion but "the texts and standards also demonstrate that students need to understand virtually nothing about religion to make sense of the world here and now."[35] In fact, he goes on to argue, "Public education leaves students religiously illiterate, it falls far short of religious neutrality, and it borders on secular indoctrination (if only unintended)."[36]

He concludes that students are illiberally educated if they only learn to think about various areas of knowledge in secular categories.

Thus, students need to understand the basics about what John Rawls called "comprehensive doctrines" or what Jean-Francois Lyotard called "metanarratives" or others call "different worldviews."[37] "Political liberalism," Rawls contends, "assumes that, for political purposes, a plurality of reasonable yet incompatible comprehensive doctrines is the normal result of the exercise of human reason within the framework of the free institutions of a constitutional democratic regime."[38]

Justice toward different religious and secular traditions of thought requires two things. First, students need to be exposed to the broad outlines of different major religious and secular intellectual traditions. Second, students need to be taught to have an empathetic understanding of what it might be like to operate within that identity tradition. Or, as Warren Nord puts it, "If we are to take religion seriously, we must take seriously religious claims to truth as *truth is understood within various religious traditions.*"[39]

Stewardship III: Caring for the Natural World

Typically, students must choose from a list of science courses and labs to fulfill their general education in this area. These classes merely introduce students to a block of knowledge or set of lab practices instead of a way of moral thinking, feeling, and acting in relation to the natural world. Yet although not everyone will be a professional scientist, all humans must develop a moral relationship to the rest of the natural world. Exploring and cultivating this moral relationship should be the focus of classes offered in this Great Identity.

In fact, how humans should interact with the rest of the natural world is one of the most important moral questions facing humans in our time. Although science classes expose students to the wonder of nature, not all of them will broach this essential, normative question. It is one thing to understand various processes that occur in the natural world or what it means to think about them from a scientific perspective; it is another thing entirely to understand oneself as a moral agent in relation to that natural world. As a result, students should be introduced to the most important morally-informed, scientific conversations about caring for the natural world.

Gender and Sexuality

Gender and sexuality are currently hot topics on any college campus because they involve identities in which everyone is invested. Moreover, such identities have been the source of legal and other forms of discrimination in America's past. Usually, these identities are the province of special interest groups in the cocurricular arena of the university. Otherwise, educational leaders leave them to certain interdisciplinary studies departments on campus.

Although such departments are important, a more human education would recognize every student's need to spend time reflecting about both the descriptive and normative issues associated with these identities. In essence, students need to think critically about how these forms of identity influence their view of the world, along with how a particular understanding of the ethical story may challenge, alter, and even deepen their appreciation of what it means to be an excellent man, woman, etc.

Moreover, although universities spend vast amounts of resources and time teaching students about sexual consent and enforcing the sexual consent ethical rule (i.e., get informed consent before sex), they spend virtually no curricular time actually educating students about moral traditions of sexual thought. Thus, instead of helping students understand identity excellence using the nine moral elements I described earlier, they simply reduce sexual education to a particular moral rule (do not engage in sexual relationships without consent).

Thus, students may never consider how the whole realm of virtue ethics might apply to sex (e.g., love, faithfulness, self-control, etc.) or other elements of identity excellence. That institutions of higher education would settle for Title IX *training* instead of sex and gender *education* demonstrates a betrayal of their educational missions.

The Third Year

By the third and fourth years, students' education should continue to turn outward to others and the beings, structures, and organizations humans create. General education classes focusing on the Great Identities should do the same.

Family, Singleness, and Marriage

One of the most important things humans create are families. The development of humans always involves developing those areas that every student will face—family relationships. This includes those that are ongoing as well as the potential families that students may or may not choose to create. A more human education would provide students with opportunities to think expansively and critically about their family relationships, the diversity of family norms, and what leads to healthy family lives.

For instance, I find that most students do not know that family stability is correlated with educational success and poverty.[40] In addition, they may not understand how decisions such as cohabitation could have implications for the well-being of their future marriage (if they decide to get married) or for their children (if they have children while cohabitating).[41] A model for this type of course can be found in a course offered at Northwestern University that teaches students the basics of what makes for healthy relationships.[42]

Stewardship IV: Culture (Two Courses)

The question of how students should interact with culture, defined simply as human creations, has been a perennial ethical question.[43] One of the most revealing types of evidence of an individual's loves is how they use their money. As such, this single component of culture is used as an illustrative example for the purposes of this text. Most majors in college discuss how to be excellent at earning money. Yet an equally important class involves exploring the question of how to spend it well. The secular university, as John Sommerville has pointed out, fails to offer answers to this question:

> The way I put it to my students is to ask where in the university they would go to learn how to *spend* their money. We have lots of programs that tell you how to make money and be useful to the economy. But where would you learn how to spend your money intelligently? That is, where does one learn what is valuable in and of itself? What is the point of money? It is not self-evident, although we increasingly treat it as such.[44]

Students usually fail to receive any help from college in this area.

The result of this failure is not very surprising. Students tend to view money as a means to happiness. Sociologist Christian Smith found more than half of eighteen to twenty-three-year-olds measure their happiness by the possessions they own (paid for by money). Almost all also saw nothing wrong with a lifestyle of mass consumerism where every desire is satisfied through a purchase. Smith shares one student's view: "I would like to have a house, a car, the American dream kind of thing, just a set-up job, decent pay kind of thing."[45] Suggesting that this view is typical, Smith then offers the following analysis: "For the most part, in thinking about what a good life is, about what their own well-lived lives should look like, when it comes specifically to buying, owning, and consuming, emerging adults did not think very expansively or critically or creatively."[46]

Addressing the failure of college students to think critically about how to spend money requires an honest evaluation of colleges. College students need to be exposed to different moral traditions that discuss different ways to think about stewarding money. They also need exposure to social scientific research in this area. For example, one of the largest studies of college students' spirituality in recent years concluded, *"One of the surest ways to enhance the spiritual development of college students is to encourage them to engage in almost any form of charitable or altruistic activity."*[47] Students need to understand how certain developmental outcomes relate to their stewardship of money.

Good Citizens

Though explored in depth in the introduction, it is worth noting again the inherently moral purposes of higher education as they relate to citizenship. Stanley Fish has argued, "No doubt, the practices of responsible citizenship and moral behavior should be encouraged in our young adults, but it's not the business of the university to do so, except when the morality in question is the morality that penalizes cheating, plagiarizing and shoddy teaching, and the desired citizenship is defined not by the demands of democracy, but by the demands of the academy."[48] As explained in the introduction, the present argument is consistent with Fish's argument in that it maintains that the approach to moral education in higher education has been corrupted by Meta-Democracy.

Still, any approach to moral education must acknowledge that, in the contemporary world, every person must be a citizen of a particular nation-state. One cannot escape to the desert away from any kingdom as the monastic tradition of various religious traditions allowed. By offering a general education on citizenship, a university would face the fact that every student must think about being a good citizen. In every course, an instructor must prioritize the intellectual traditions to which it exposes students, and this course would be no different. Since most universities are government-funded, it should be no surprise that they prioritize some form of the American liberal-democratic story and identity. Of course, other identities can orient the approach to citizenship.

Such a course should also be liberal in looking at the practice of citizenship in a holistic fashion. Recognizing the importance of the narrative—or worldview—in shaping one's conception of citizenship and its ends requires exploring the whole range of virtues and vices associated with citizenship (and not merely procedural forms of justice, for example, or courage in the context of one national or political story). In doing so, the course should expose students to a range of practices, models, and wisdom associated with being a good citizen.

Senior Year: Capstone on Being Good Human Beings

The old moral philosophy capstone course provided in early American colleges sought to help students bring together their learning from all four years. This senior capstone course would attempt to do the same but in a different way. It would strive to help students think about how to combine the pursuit of identity excellence in all areas of their lives into one flourishing life. Similar to the first-year course on human flourishing offered at the University of Virginia, although at a more advanced level, this course would explore how people combine identity excellence in different areas, along with how to sort through moral conflicts when the pursuit of excellence between identities comes into conflict (the subject of the last chapters of this book).

ADDRESSING A FEW MORE CRITICISMS

Courses on Being a Good Friend, a Good Spouse, or Good Neighbor Would Be Too Easy

Anyone who has had difficulties with friends, marriage, or neighbors knows that being excellent in these endeavors is hard. Why do we think then that a class covering these subjects would be easy? The difficulty of such a course would largely depend upon the level of reading material. For instance, the readings I mentioned earlier, Aristotle's chapter on friendship in the *Nicomachean Ethics*, Robert Putnam's *Bowling Alone*, and Martin Luther King Jr.'s sermon "Loving Your Enemy," are all significant readings that would and should challenge and engage first-year students.

Will Students Learn Competencies that Accrediting Agencies Require?

This is the primary question of every administrator. Most competencies can be taught in any course. The problem is that developing good human beings requires teaching students to acquire and exercise competencies, such as critical moral thinking, in the context of something that is relevant and influential to their thoughts, loves, and behaviors throughout their lives.

Changing All of General Education Would Be Impractical or Too Much Work

All change is challenging, but the suggestions here are not impractical. However, they are unappealing (i.e., too much work) to a tenured professor comfortable within their established system. Consequently, any committee seeking to make these changes should be stacked with young assistant professors who have not become lazy and corrupted by the current spoils system. Most general education courses are taught by these young professors anyway.

Such Courses Will Be Biased or Indoctrinating

Critics may raise the concern that such courses would be biased or involve indoctrination. Of course, any decision about how to structure the curriculum involves preference for one identity or another, but the curriculum always—even as it presently exists—represents an ordering of priorities. In addition, general education courses exploring various ways of understanding what it means to be a good friend or good citizen would not necessarily be indoctrinating or limited. After all, a diversity of answers to these issues exists both inside and outside various moral traditions.

CONCLUSION

Overall, academics who dream and talk about a "better way" must start by creating revolutions where they work. They need to heed the call for radical change on behalf of students oppressed by general education everywhere. General education dissidents of the world unite! Unite not to change the political structures of the world—that would be far too easy. No, unite to do something more daring and more futile. Rage against all the vested professional interests in the academy. Ask educational leaders to do something radical, even if it involves more work. And, take curricular chances for the good of the students we claim to serve. Do so knowing the reward is worthwhile: instead of diminishing ourselves, we can enrich our selves.

NOTES

1. Frederick Rudolph, *Curriculum, A History of the American Undergraduate Course of Study since 1636* (San Francisco: Jossey-Bass, 1977), 1.

2. John Dewey, *The School and Society* (Chicago: University of Chicago Press, 1899), 34.

3. Joshua Eyler, *How Humans Learn: The Science and Stories Behind Effective College Teaching* (Morgantown: West Virginia University Press, 2018); James M. Lang, *Cheating Lessons: Learning from Academic Dishonesty* (Cambridge, MA: Harvard University Press, 2013).

4. Hanstedt does propose addressing a similar possible theme in general education. Yet Hanstedt's answer to addressing this theme is for students to choose from a list of distribution requirements across a variety of disciplines. The inclusion of this category is not driven by a moral vision. Paul Hanstedt, *General Education Essentials: A Guide for College Faculty* (San Francisco: John Wiley & Sons, 2012), 29–31.

5. Dewey, *The School and Society*, 51.

6. Christian Smith with Kari Christoffersen, Hilary Davidson, and Patricia Snell Herzog, *Lost in Transition: The Dark Side of Emerging Adulthood* (New York: Oxford University Press, 2011).

7. Irene Clark, "Genre, Identity, and the Brain: Insights from Neuropsychology," *Journal of General Education* 65, no 1 (2016): 1–19.

8. Clark, "Genre, Identity, and the Brain," 13–14.

9. The recent emphasis upon linked courses for general education and integrative learning provides evidence of this realization. See Margot Soven, Dolores Lehr, Siskanna Naynaha, and Wendy Olson, Linked Courses for General Education and Integrative Learning: A Guide for Faculty and Administrators (Sterling, VA: Stylus Publishing, 2013).

10. Kwame Anthony Appiah, *Experiments in Ethics* (Cambridge, MA: Harvard University Press, 2008); James M. Lang, *Cheating Lessons: Learning from Academic Dishonesty* (Cambridge, MA: Harvard University Press, 2013), 175–78.

11. For a critique of this failure to focus upon excellence see Anthony Kronman, *The Assault on American Excellence* (New York: Free Press, 2019).

12. Eyler, *How Humans Learn*; Lang, *Cheating Lessons*.

13. Vimal Pitel, "Why Colleges Are Keeping a Closer Eye on Their Students' Lives," *The Chronicle of Higher Education*, February 18, 2019, https://www.chronicle.com/interactives/Trend19-InLoco-Main?cid=wcontentgrid_2Trends.

14. Pitel, "Why Colleges Are Keeping a Closer Eye on Their Students' Lives."

15. Christine Gross-Loh, "The First Lesson of Marriage 101: There Are No Soul Mates," *The Atlantic*, February 2014, https://www.theatlantic.com/education/archive/2014/02/the-first-lesson-of-marriage-101-there-are-no-soul-mates/283712/.

16. Beckie Supiano, "Colleges Teach Students How to Think. Should They Also Teach Them How to Thrive?" *The Chronicle of Higher Education*, November 4, 2018, https://www.chronicle.com/article/colleges-teach-students-how-to-think-should-they-also-teach-them-how-to-thrive/.

17. University of North Carolina at Chapel Hill "Adulting 101," UNC.edu, accessed April 10, 2020, https://library.unc.edu/house/workshops/adulting-101/.

18. University of Denver, "Adulting 101," DU.edu, accessed April 10, 2020, https://www.du.edu/health-and-counseling-center/healthpromotion/mental_health/adulting101.html.

19. George D. Kuh et al., *Student Success in College: Creating Conditions That Matter* (San Francisco: Jossey-Bass, 2010). This oft-cited text on student success defines success as "higher-than-predicted graduation rates and better-than-predicted student engagement scores on the NSSE" (xii). For a more in-depth discussion of the instrumentalism of institution-down approaches to student success interventions see Theodore F. Cockle, "Morally Animated: Toward a First-Year Seminar from the Person Up," *Journal of College and Character* 20, no. 3 (2019): 218–33.

20. Cockle, "Morally Animated," 225.

21. Perry L. Glanzer, Jonathan P. Hill, and Byron R. Johnson, *The Quest for Purpose: The Collegiate Search for a Meaningful Life* (Albany: State University of New York Press, 2017).

22. Robert D. Putnam, *Bowling Alone: The Collapse and Revival of American Community* (New York: Simon & Schuster, 2000).

23. Jason S. Baehr, *The Inquiring Mind on Intellectual Virtues and Virtue Epistemology* (New York: Oxford University Press, 2011). See also Jason S. Baehr, *Intellectual Virtues and Education: Essays in Applied Virtue Epistemology* (New York: Routledge, Taylor & Francis Group, 2016).

24. Personal interviews from the Baylor Faith and Character study. For more about the study see Kevin Dougherty, Perry L. Glanzer, Sarah Schnitker, Juliette Ratchford, and Jessica Robinson, "Baylor Faith and Character Study: Methods and Preliminary Findings," *Christian Higher Education* (2021): https://doi.org/10.1080/15363759.2021.1929564.

25. Donald L. McCabe, Linda K. Treviño, and Kenneth D. Butterfield, *Cheating in College: Why Students Do It and What Educators Can Do About It* (Baltimore, MD: Johns Hopkins University Press, 2012).

26. Jason S. Baehr, *The Inquiring Mind on Intellectual Virtues and Virtue Epistemology* (New York: Oxford University Press, 2011). See also Jason S. Baehr, *Intellectual Virtues and Education: Essays in Applied Virtue Epistemology* (New York: Routledge, Taylor & Francis Group, 2016).

27. Cockle, "Morally Animated," 218–33.

28. Studies show the transition from high school to college leads to troubling declines in physical activity, nutrition, and sleep. Studies also show troubling levels of stress, anxiety, loneliness, depression, weight-gain, sexual promiscuity, and heavy alcohol use among college students. For more details see American College Health Association, "American College Health Association-National College Health Assessment II: Undergraduate Student Reference Group Executive Summary, Spring 2015" (Hanover, MD: American College Health Association, 2015); Cynthia M. Ferrara, "The College Experience: Physical Activity, Nutrition, and Implications for Intervention and Future Research," *Journal of Exercise Physiology* 12, no. 1 (2009): 23–35; Kathryn Silliman, Kathleen Rodas-Fortier, and Michelle Neyman, "A Survey of Dietary and Exercise Habits and Perceived Barriers to Following a Healthy Lifestyle in a College Population," *Californian Journal of Health Promotion* 2, no. 2 (2004): 10; and Toben F. Nelson et al., "Vigorous Physical Activity Among College Students in the United States," *Journal of Physical Activity and Health* 4, no. 4 (October 2007): 496–509, https://doi.org/10.1123/jpah.4.4.496.

29. Ferrara, "The College Experience."

30. Smith, *Lost in Transition*.

31. See for example Jennifer Beste, *College Hookup Culture and Christian Ethics: The Lives and Longings of Emerging Adults* (New York: Oxford University Press, 2017).

32. George Yancey, "An Abusive Relationship and Race Relations," http://www.patheos.com/blogs/shatteringparadigms/2018/04/an-abusive-relationship-and-race-relations/.

33. Yancey, "An Abusive Relationship and Race Relations."

34. Charles Taylor, *A Secular Age* (Cambridge, MA: Harvard University Press, 2007).

35. Warren A. Nord, *Does God Make a Difference? Taking Religion Seriously in Our Schools and Universities* (Oxford: Oxford University Press, 2010), 60.

36. Nord, *Does God Make a Difference?*, 99.

37. John Rawls, *Political Liberalism* (New York: Columbia University Press, 1996); Jean-Francois Lyotard, *The Postmodern Condition: A Report on Knowledge*, trans. Brian Massumi (Minneapolis: University of Minnesota Press, 1985); David Naugle, *Worldview: The History of a Concept* (Grand Rapids, MI: Eerdmans, 2002).

38. John Rawls, *Political Liberalism*, xviii.

39. Warren A. Nord, *Religion and American Education* (Chapel Hill: University of North Carolina Press, 2014), 221.

40. Raj Chetty, Nathaniel Hendren, Patrick Kline, and Emmanuel Saez, "Where Is the Land of Opportunity? The Geography of Intergenerational Mobility in the United States," *The Quarterly Journal of Economics* 129, no. 4 (November 2014): 1553–1623, https://doi.org/10.1093/qje/qju022; Thomas DeLeire and Leonard M. Lopoo, "Family Structure and the Economic Mobility of Children," Pew Economic Mobility Project, https://www.pewtrusts.org/-/media/legacy/uploadedfiles/pcs_assets /2010/familystructurepdf.pdf.

41. Michael J. Rosenfeld and Katherina Roesler, "Cohabitation Experience and Cohabitation's Association with Marital Dissolution," *Journal of Marriage and Family* 81, no. 1 (February 2019): 42–58; Scott M. Stanley, Galena K. Rhoades, Paul R. Amato, Howard J. Markman, and Christine A. Johnson, "The Timing of Cohabitation and Engagement: Impact on First and Second Marriages," *Journal of Marriage and Family* 72, no. 4 (2010) 906; Scott M. Stanley, Galena K. Rhoades, and Frank D. Fincham, "Understanding Romantic Relationships among Emerging Adults: The Significant Roles of Cohabitation and Ambiguity," in *Romantic Relationships in Emerging Adulthood*, eds. Frank D. Fincham and Ming Cui (New York: Cambridge University Press, 2011), 234–51; Scott M. Stanley, Galena K. Rhoades, and Howard J. Markman, "Sliding vs. Deciding: Inertia and the Premarital Cohabitation Effect." *Family Relations*, 55 (2006): 499–509.

42. Christine Gross-Loh, "The First Lesson of Marriage 101: There Are No Soul Mates."

43. H. Richard Niebuhr, *Christ and Culture* (New York: Harper, 1956).

44. C. John Sommerville, *The Decline of the Secular University* (New York: Oxford, 2008), 8.

45. Smith, *Lost in Transition*, 100.

46. Smith, *Lost in Transition*, 100.

47. Alexander W. Astin, Helen S. Astin, and Jennifer A. Lindholm. *Cultivating the Spirit: How College Can Enhance Students' Inner Lives* (San Francisco: Jossey-Bass, 2011), 147 (italics in original).

48. Fish, *Save the World on Your Own Time* (New York: Oxford University Press, 2008), 67.

Chapter 8

Identity Prioritization and Integration for Excellence

Fundamentally, personal identity is a matter of what we care about in the world. . . . Eventually, our emergent *personal identity* is a matter of how we prioritize one concern as our "ultimate concern" and how we subordinate but yet accommodate others to it.

—Margaret S. Archer[1]

What identity or set of identities is most important to you? It is one of life's most important questions. The ordering of loves and identities has long been a theological and philosophical discussion, and it continues to receive scrutiny in these disciplines. For example, it received fresh expression through the work of philosopher Harry Frankfurt. In a 1988 volume, Frankfurt argued that we need a new section of philosophy that focuses upon "*what to care about.*"[2]

Frankfurt defined "caring" by contrasting it with ethics:

Ethics focuses on the problem of ordering our relations with *other people*. It is concerned especially with the contrast between *right* and *wrong*, and with the grounds and limits of *moral obligation*. We are led into the third branch of inquiry, on the other hand, because we are interested in deciding what to do with *ourselves* and because we therefore need to understand what is *important*, or, rather, what is *important to us*.[3]

In contrast to Frankfurt's differentiation between ethics and "importance," most theologians rely on an Augustinian approach to the ordering of loves (including love of self, others, and divine) that considers our cares/affections within the realm of ethics. After all, the reality is that as we live, we all make choices about what identities, and the moral cultures of excellence associated with those identities, are most important in our own lives.

135

The time spent practicing how to be a good professor can clash with the time needed to practice being a good father or mother. One can experience a clash between virtues such as loyalty to one's country and loyalty to one's religion or family. Certain students may face an ethical conflict between finishing their college degree and responding to a family crisis at home. We face choices between prioritizing God or the self. For instance, the practice of resting from work one day a week can conflict with certain views about what it means to be an excellent professional.

Frankfurt would never have needed to distinguish between ethics and "caring" if modernity had not reduced ethics to issues of right and wrong instead of also including what it means to be good or bad. Modern thinking tended to focus on following moral principles instead of striving for identity excellence.

Striving for excellence quickly makes apparent the reality that moral conflict continually occurs in multiple forms over the course of a lifetime. As chapter 3 notes, people face this issue every day, asking questions like: Should I be a good professional and work more on this lecture for work or spend time with my wife and kids? Individuals are constantly faced with the question of how to integrate all these competing selves, desires, and loves. Rather than emphasizing universal rights and wrongs (as modernity suggests), the most *fundamental* ethical dilemmas relate to determining how to order our loves and figuring out how to prioritize and integrate our identities.

In fact, almost all moral conflict is a conflict between two or more of our identities. Can one really be a student-athlete? Can one be a practicing gay Muslim? Can one be a good citizen and a religious pacifist? There is clearly a need to engage in values clarification regarding identities. Of course, the problem with the old values clarification movement was that it avoided the fact that such conflicts occur at a variety of levels, and its promoters acted as if humans have not been engaged in this process since the dawn of humanity. In fact, students come to the university already engaged in this process.

This chapter describes this student starting point and then describes what identity excellence development regarding identity conflict would look like in different kinds of colleges.

AN EXAMPLE FROM A FIRST-YEAR STUDENT

Samuel, a first-year premed student, arrived at college with a set of moral resources that would be typical for his age group. He shared, "If I really need guidance on moral counsel, I turn to my parents." In addition, he looked to family members as his moral heroes, although the heroism of his parents and grandparents was certainly special:

One of them is definitely my mother. When she went through [pause]. She's a nurse now, but when she went to nursing school, she said that she had it rough. This was back when she was the first—the only rather—Black lady to graduate in her nursing program. And she went through a lot of adversity. One of her professors actually told her that she could find any nurse better on the street than her. And she overcame it all and became a nurse. And she's actually looking to go back and get her doctorate in nursing practice. So, she's one of the greatest of them all that I really look up to. And then my grandmother too. She was one of the only Blacks in her class too. And that was during the segregation times, and she definitely overcame a lot, went through a lot. So, both of them are really big in my life.

In addition to the guidance and inspiration of his parents, he also looked to his religious tradition for moral help. He shared, "Most of the times, I'll turn to prayer and the Bible for some help." He gave us an example of how his search for moral guidance in the Bible shaped his life. "I'm Catholic. So, I try to live by the beatitudes each day. Specifically, 'Blessed are the Peacemakers for they shall be called sons of God,' and 'Blessed are the merciful for they shall be shown mercy.'"

The last one, in particular, helped guide him through times of anger. He shared his approach: "I'm not gonna be angry with you for a long time. I'll eventually forgive you, and we can go back to being friends." Samuel's recognition of the importance of the moral virtues of mercy and forgiveness seems commonplace until one compares his experience to those who grew up amidst other moral traditions lacking an imagination for forgiveness as a virtue.[4] For Samuel, both his moral heroes and the Christian scriptures reinforced a certain kind of grit in the face of life's challenges.

As a high school student, Samuel had already faced some moral challenges. These moral challenges had to do with choosing how to integrate competing identity priorities in his life and his efforts to be excellent in both:

So, I was the first student body president and drum major at the same time. And the band directors did not want me to do my student body president job at all. So, it came out to be—what should I do? Should I just give up and not do a student body president side? Should I stop doing the drum major side, so I can make more of one? So, it was one or the other. So, what I did was, I said, "You know what?" I started to [pause] what's the word I'm looking for? Dedicate, not really dedicate, but give time to each of them. Not just one. I gave time to this one for a little while and I gave time to that one for a little while so that I could be effective in both.

Unfortunately, some of the adults in his life, who should have been helping him, actually resisted his efforts to be excellent in multiple endeavors.

Granted, they probably saw themselves as providing him with practical wisdom about how to manage competing identity demands for excellence.

This decision to resist the desires of his band leaders started to take a toll on him emotionally and physically He said, "My band directors were telling me that they didn't want me to do these things. They didn't want me to do that. They were just kind of all coming down on me and just were down. . . . And they made my life a lot worse. And I actually lost twenty pounds from that stress." Unfortunately, Samuel paid a significant price for resisting what he perceived to be the desires of adults who underestimated his capabilities.

Yet during this difficult time he found sources of strength. "So, I started to pray even more. So, the Bible, prayer, and church—I found a lot of refuge there." Indeed, this source of strength came from the whole Christian tradition and community. He said,

> I started to talk to my pastor a lot more. And I found that through confirmation classes and talking to my priest and talking to the counselors, talking to the peer ministry leader—that all helped me. And then reading the Bible itself, specifically psalms—that helped me a lot to get through everything that I needed to get through. And I found that those people were really instrumental. And a lot of my teachers, too, were instrumental and made sure that I was okay, so I could be successful in everything that I did.

He ended up succeeding and acquiring wisdom that he did not have before—it was a wisdom that he was able to share with his graduating class:

> The wisdom I have acquired is "never give up." I came by that because after this year and previous years too, I wanted to give up a lot of times. And I remember some of the quotes when I gave at my graduation speech—that was one of the quotes that I used. And I believe it was by Vince Lombardi. And it was like, "Never give up. You should never give up." And I looked at my mom and what she came through and she never gave up. And I looked at my grandmother and what she went through, and she never gave up. And I looked at my dad, what he goes through. He never gives up. So, the moral of the story is never give up because no matter how hard it gets, you can always come through. And I always look to the Bible too. And the Lord never said that anything was gonna be easy. So, you always have to push through it no matter what.

Samuel exhibited what scholars today celebrate as grit.[5] He demonstrated grit through his high school experience with the help of wise mentors, helpful models, and a larger community of character rooted in the Christian tradition.

Ultimately, it is this Christian faith that now gives his life meaning as he begins his college career. In other words, like most students, Samuel is not going to college to find meaning. He believes he already has a source of meaning:

> What gives my life meaning is to know that I have somebody always at my side. Anytime that I need something I can always turn to somebody. And that somebody is God. Anytime, I know that God will never leave nor forsake me. He will always be there to help me through no matter how hard times get. And what makes life worth living is because I know that I'm loved by everybody, and God loves me. And I know I love God. And then my parents love me, and I see the love of God through everybody that I talk to. So that's what makes life worth living and why I love.

To say that Samuel is self-authoring his moral life at this point would be inaccurate. Instead, Samuel is already engaged in coauthoring his life in a way that involves actively ordering and merging his identities, which he is doing with the help of a common metaidentity and metanarrative and his moral mentors. Of course, he also had to resist well-meaning educators who did not account for his longings and desires.

IDENTITY EXCELLENCE DEVELOPMENT IN COLLEGE

Moral education in higher education, as suggested in the previous chapter, would not try to separate Samuel from his previous moral mentors in the name of fostering self-authorship. Instead, it would seek to make Samuel aware of the increasing complexity of his quest for excellence in his Great Identities. Furthermore, it would equip him with the tools to be conscious of how to continue ordering and merging one's identities in a coherent way.

When young emerging adults like Samuel enter college, they face an increasing array of choices regarding how to understand themselves as moral actors who choose among and prioritize their various identities. Sociologist Margaret Archer has explored and described this process in a somewhat similar way. She maintained, "Since *personal identity* derives from subjects' interactions with the world, its natural, practical and social orders, it is dependent upon the prior experience of a *sense of self*. The latter secures the fact that the three orders of reality are all impinging on the same subject—who also knows it."[6]

Similarly, the theory presented in this book maintains that a student's sense of self is developed in interaction with nature, the moral frameworks associated with the Great Identities provided by society, and transcendent traditions of moral thought. A university education should help students unpack the unique identities in the context of the interplay of the natural order, the Great

Identities, the transcendent, and their burgeoning sense of self. As Archer mentions in the opening quote, "Fundamentally, *personal identity* is a matter of what we care about in the world."[7]

An education in the Great Identities helps students discover, understand, and build their personal identity. Human beings must establish excellent relations with nature, human culture, their profession, their family, their friends and enemies, their country, their neighbors, the metaphysical world, and more if they hope to flourish. Merely teaching them to be excellent citizens or professionals alone will not help them survive and thrive in the other identity areas.

At times, the moral cultures of these identities will clash as we pursue identity excellence. For example, in her book *Moving Up without Losing Your Way*, Jennifer Morton tells the story of Kimberly, a Harvard MBA student who had lost her father when she was two. Raised by her mother and grandmother, a Barbados immigrant, she shared how she prioritized her identities compared to other Americans:

> I think Americans are a lot more individualistic. I would never put my mother in a nursing home. She would live with me. She was living with me in Texas after she lost her job. It's not a question. You know, I've had friends try to say "Oh, you don't have to do this." No, I don't think so. You take care of your family. That's number one. I wouldn't be where I am if my family . . . didn't put all their money together and were house-poor so I could get an education.[8]

Here we see a student make a clear assessment of how she orders her identities (family over the Meta-Democratic virtue of autonomy) and the reasons for them. In this case, it stems from gratitude and loyalty.

Furthermore, as Jennifer Morton points out throughout her book, this kind of identity conflict is particularly acute for low-income students, who she labels "strivers," who must interact with the dominant culture:

> What hasn't been adequately appreciated is that some of the most important sacrifices strivers make are *ethical*, that is, they concern the most meaningful and valuable aspects of a good life. What is potentially on the line is not just money, time, or hard work, but their relationships with friends and family, the bonds they have with their community, and sometimes even their sense of identity.[9]

It is worth adding that students from any minority culture (e.g., racial, religious, geographic, gender, family, etc.) may experience this tension, a bifurcated state between two identities.

Morton points out that one cannot and should not resolve these types of identity conflict by just acting in one identity context and then being authentic in another context (i.e., moral code-switching). The reason is that we often end up acquiring the particular virtues prized in an "acting" identity context even if we are acting. She shares how she picked up what is considered a virtue in philosophy—being sharp and argumentative—and then applied it to other parts of her life, even though she saw herself as merely acting the part in class.

In reality, when it comes to a conflict between one's two identities, one will eventually have to choose. Morton notes, "Your 'family self' may think you should go visit your grandmother, while your 'work self' may think you should stay at work, but which self is the one who is going to decide?"[10] Morton argues that individuals must strive for integrity and wholeness by learning to prioritize identities and moral traditions of excellence. Consequently, there will be instances where certain identities are allowed to take priority over others. She writes,

> The ethical challenge lies in striking a balance between resisting the pressure to adopt the dominant cultural norms when those conflict with our values and being flexible enough to adapt and thrive in that culture. As we have seen, neither dividing the self nor pretending is a viable strategy. What we need is a way to codeswitch that allows us to be clear about what matters to us. . . . When there is so much pressure to fit in in order to succeed, taking control of those aspects of our identity that matter to us requires reflection.[11]

This reality confirms the need for education regarding excellence in the Great Identities that includes helping students reflect upon how to prioritize the Great Identities in all the Great Identity courses, but especially in the senior capstone course. What Morton claims about the narrative of strivers is actually true of all people: "First, it affirms a plurality of ethical goods that matters to one's life—one's relationships, culture, and connection to one's community—rather than focusing only on educational or economic achievement."[12] In fact, Morton, arguably, does not go far enough. People inhabit numerous identity cultures and communities (plural).

She goes on to note, "Second, it makes it clear that some of those ethical goods will have to be traded off or sacrificed for the sake of other goods and opportunities."[13] In other words, students must order their affections or loves with regard to these identities. They must determine why they care about certain identity relationships more than others. After all, when a moral conflict occurs, it is more than likely to be a result of their efforts to be excellent in their identities. The conflict does not arise if someone cares little about a particular identity (e.g., being a Rhode Islander, half Austrian, white, libertarian, etc.). It is only in striving to be excellent in more than one identity that moral conflict occurs.

Archer makes a similar point, although she uses the term "concerns" instead of "affections." She notes, "[W]hat precise balance we strike between our concerns and what precisely figures among a subject's constellation of concerns is what give us our strict identities as *particular persons*. Eventually, our emergent *personal identity* is a matter of how we prioritize one concern as our 'ultimate concern' and how we subordinate but yet accommodate others to it"[14]

In other words, a unique ordering of identities is one of the things that makes each human being unique (and not simply general citizens or professionals). By reprioritizing concerns (personal identity) to refute/change various social identities, people maintain personal agency even as they are social actors. Integration and prioritization occur upon choosing a metaidentity, narrative, and purpose. The moral elements of this metaidentity then shape and even transform other moral identities. The virtues one develops as a loving mother or an obedient Muslim or free-thinking atheist, for example, will then shape how one engages in being excellent in one's profession or citizenship.

The prioritization of the Great Identities is an ongoing process throughout life, and it involves a person's whole being—affections, emotions, will, and behavior. It is not something that is accomplished once and for all, although there are certainly moments for making key decisions (e.g., marriage, taking a job, deciding to care for a parent, becoming a citizen, a religious conversion or de-conversion, starting or cutting off a friendship, having children, etc.).

Still, even these kinds of major outlooks and decisions are subject to some degree of revision. As Archer notes, the essence of being an individual human with a personal identity involves a person conducting "an endless assessment of whether what it once devoted itself to as its ultimate concern is still worthy of this devotion and whether or not the price once paid for subordinating and accommodating other concerns is still one with which the subject can live."[15] Thus, one of the first things that higher education should do is to educate students to engage in this type of identity prioritization assessment. A university's type informs how it might help students.

THE PLURALISTIC, REDUCTIVE COMPREHENSIVE, AND IMAGO DEI UNIVERSITY

One of the helpful but challenging features of undertaking this prioritization and integration of identities in universities pertains to the general identities of three types of universities: pluralistic universities, reductive comprehensive universities (e.g., Meta-Democratic universities), and humanizing universities. All three are morally formative and can engage in teaching identity excellence, prioritization, and integration, but they also have key differences when it comes to how they encourage students to prioritize and merge their identities.

Pluralistic Universities

Pertaining to moral formation, a pluralistic university relies on thin forms of agreement about what it means to be an excellent human. As a result, pluralistic universities focus on identity excellence elements by creating a moral culture with these eight moral elements: (1) an educational and perhaps civic identity and narrative; (2) an educational purpose (e.g., mission statement); (3) rules for university and professional life (e.g., student handbook and classes teaching professional ethics); (4) identified intellectual, moral, civic, and performance virtues for professional excellence and for living life in a pluralistic nation and community (e.g., academic honesty, self-control, justice, autonomy); (5) practices for developing these virtues (e.g., projects, exams, opportunities for service, and advocacy for social justice, etc.); (6) mentors for specific forms of professional and civic identity excellence (e.g., what it means to be a good biologist); (7) models of specific forms of excellence (e.g., what it means to be an excellent alum, professional, citizen, etc.); and (8) practical wisdom for specific forms of excellence.

The strength of the pluralistic intellectual context is a lack of a specific vision for human flourishing and a wide amount of diversity. This combination allows for greater autonomy, certain kinds of creativity, and the development of intellectual humility that comes from sharpening one's ideas through engagement with diverse perspectives about identity excellence and identity ordering. Ideally, in this setting, students experience a wide-ranging tournament of metaidentities and metanarratives competing for their vision of the good life among faculty equipped to help students navigate this tournament in intellectually honest ways. In addition, they also emphasize widely recognized virtues on which there is broad agreement, such as intellectual honesty, service, and social justice.

Pluralistic University Limits

The limit of pluralistic universities is that the moral education they provide rarely extends beyond these commonalities. Thus, it is not surprising that the most recent major study of exemplary moral education in higher education was criticized for relying too heavily upon religious, ethnic, or military institutions—referred to here as imago Dei and reductive comprehensive universities. These are schools where "a certain homogeneity of culture is the advertised point of the enterprise."[16] The critique leveled against Colby et al. neglects the fact that around the time of the study virtually all higher education institutions identified by the Templeton Foundation as moral education exemplars were either private religious colleges and universities or military academies.[17]

In truth, with a few exceptions, pluralistic universities have tended to avoid emphasizing virtue development outside of professional or civic contexts.[18] Thus, they can and do help students form the character and virtues necessary to be good intellectuals, professionals, and citizens, but the range of shared rationales for doing so will be more limited. In their effort to focus on human commonalities, they may limit their pluralism. Consequently, they often do not address broader forms of character development involving excellence in other identities (e.g., what virtues are required to be an excellent spouse, parent, friend, Muslim, Jew, etc.).

Finally, such institutions do not provide an agreed upon metaidentity and metanarrative that would more clearly define the virtues and order the importance of identities in conflict (e.g., conflicts between the moral demands required to be an excellent spouse and an excellent professional); in fact, they often exclude certain metaidentities and narratives.[19]

The Danger of Purposelessness

The danger of not providing a metanarrative capable of establishing a metaidentity can lead to increased student purposelessness.[20] Consider one student, Erin. By all accounts, Erin would appear to be a clear success story. A minority student who overcame an extremely difficult family background to attend an Ivy League institution, she saw herself as someone who set goals and achieved them. She confessed to one of my colleagues, however, "I'm the kind of person that if I don't have some sort of an end goal, it's just really hard for me to motivate myself to do anything." Erin had such end goals in high school and the support needed to reach them. She recalls, "In high school I just kind of chugged through it, you know, you have more of a structure, and it was easier."

Unfortunately, Erin, open about how her experience changed after arriving to college shared, "I had no sense of motivation, no sense of what I wanted to study, and I had no interest in going to class, and so I ended up saying, 'Okay, I can't do this.'" The core of the problem, she admits, came from "a lack of a sense of meaning," which manifested itself in different ways. "I was struggling with an eating disorder throughout high school and so that had been getting serious—and I think that's also linked with a lack of a sense of meaning," she reflected.

Unfortunately, Erin did not find help from her university and eventually spiraled into depression. She shared the consequence: "I took that year off to recover from my eating disorder and my depression, and to search for a sense of meaning." Erin, by her own account, was purposeless. Even worse, she did not see herself as on a journey to discover a purpose or set of purposes during her college experience. The university was not helping Erin find and order her identities and affections.[21]

Fortunately, that was not the end of Erin's story. At the time we interviewed Erin during her senior year, through the influence of mentoring—first through off-campus groups and later a religious group on-campus—she had found what she described as her particular calling and purpose. She now wanted to "go into some sort of a clinical setting where I could talk to people because I guess it has to do with my personal struggles, too, but I just, I want to be able to counsel people in some way. . . . So that's how I got interested in counseling, psychology."

In fact, she was writing her senior thesis on attitudes toward suicide within her ethnic group. Overall, the support she discovered *outside* the university helped nurture her purpose. In turn, it gave her academic direction and a sense of vocation. She also moved from being incapacitated by her own struggles to embracing a purpose that contributed to both her own flourishing and that of others.

Erin would have been helped by a general education that discussed the meaning of being excellent in the Great Identities. At the very least, students like Erin need a curricular or cocurricular course such as Search for the Good Life or Human Flourishing that does the following two things: (a) explores the different conceptions about good identity roles in the sophisticated way; and (b) explores how one achieves excellence in an identity role and then prioritizes various identities in the midst of moral conflicts—thus creating a meaningful and excellent human life (the proposed senior capstone course).

This practice would then be enhanced by exposing students to models or expert practitioners of various identity roles and resolvers of identity conflicts. After all, students need coaches/mentors who can give them insight into these roles and how to order them in life. Students would then be able, at least, to understand moral conflicts, what they are, and what they entail at all moral levels. Students would also be taught to think about life's purpose in more expansive ways. Best of all, universities might actually educate students about ethics in more sophisticated ways.

Educating about Purpose and Identity Prioritization

In a pluralistic university, a liberal education about identity prioritization in a capstone course should involve at least two key components. First, it would start by exposing students to the variety of identity prioritizations that people make—what they choose as their guiding purpose. A national study of purpose found that students who prioritize certain purposes can be separated into four types: the purposeless; the self-achievers (who desire happiness, experiences, career success, comfort, self-exploration, creating, and/or money); the relationalists (who desire family, friends, and to help others); and the transcendents (who desire to make the world better, to love God, and/or to serve their country and/or community).[22]

An education about identity prioritization could involve introducing students to the four broad types, asking in which of these they best fit, and then encouraging them to evaluate the types. The hope would be that this kind of liberal arts exposure to different identity prioritization categories, as well as other students' reasons for choosing or rejecting different identity prioritizations, would provide a kind of introductory liberal arts education to identity prioritization.

Second, students can only understand and evaluate a particular way of ordering their identities and integrating the pursuit of identity excellence by examining someone's whole life.[23] Thus, one of the major objectives of the senior capstone course would be exposing students to various narratives exemplifying the best examples of students pursuing identity excellence with an identity ordering from at least the three general categories (individual achiever; relationalists; transcendent). In this way, students could be introduced to particular ways of ordering and integrating their identities.

Yet even if students take such a class—one that provides them historical and empirical exposure to different ways to prioritize their identities—an important question remains: Should universities ever encourage particular ways of ordering and merging one's identities? Perhaps a different kind of university is required to engage this kind of modeling.

Reductive Comprehensive Universities

The second type of university—reductive comprehensive—provides education that sets forth a particular vision of human flourishing rooted in a specific identity. However, the identity inherently cannot include all humans and it is often political (e.g., a university in a communist country, a military academy), ethnic or racial (e.g., the three exemplar institutions cited in *Educating Citizens*: Turtle Mountain Community College, Tusculum College, and Spelman College), or gender-oriented (a male or female college).

The most dangerous version are the politically reductive universities, since they can be especially authoritative and indoctrinating and, in those cases, ineffective. One finds this approach to moral education in communist or other totalitarian countries.[24] Yet even reductive comprehensive universities in liberal democracies can be morally myopic. In fact, this point as been one of the major arguments of this book.

Many supposedly pluralistic universities in the United States are actually on their way to becoming reductive comprehensive universities of the political type. Although university professors in the United States are almost universally resistant to reducing the purpose of higher education to getting a job or helping the economy, they often fail to realize a slow shift toward political citizenship or professional affiliation similarly reduces the purpose of education.

The Humanizing University

In contrast to these segmented views of the self, consider visions that focus on our broad human identity. Paulo Friere argues in *Pedagogy of the Oppressed* that humanization should be the primary goal of education.[25] Similarly, the United Nations Declaration of Human Rights states, "Education shall be directed to the full development of the human personality and to the strengthening of respect for human rights and fundamental freedoms."[26] The difficulty with Friere's proposal or the first part of the UN statement is that great disagreement exists about what "humanization" or "the full development of the human personality" entails. Thus, to ensure fairness, liberal democracies can and should only fund pluralistic universities (or all the different types of universities). The final chapter maintains that one type of university, though beginning from a controversial metaphysical identity, ultimately enriches and does not reduce a shared humanity.

NOTES

1. Margaret S. Archer, "Morphogenesis: Realism's Explanatory Framework" in *Sociological Realism*, eds. A. Maccarini, E. Morandi, and R. Prandini (New York: Routledge, 2011), 89.

2. Harry G. Frankfurt, *The Importance of What We Care About: Philosophical Essays.* (Cambridge University Press, 1988), 80 (emphasis in original).

3. Frankfurt, *The Importance of What We Care About*, 80–81 (emphasis in original).

4. Perry L. Glanzer, *The Quest for Russia's Soul: Evangelicals and Moral Education in Post-Communist Russia* (Waco, TX: Baylor University Press, 2002).

5. Angela Duckworth, *Grit: The Power of Passion and Perseverance* (New York: Scribner, 2016).

6. Archer, "Morphogenesis," 88 (italics in original); Jennifer M. Morton, *Moving Up without Losing Your Way: The Ethical Costs of Upward Mobility* (Princeton, NJ: Princeton University Press, 2019), 19.

7. Archer, "Morphogenesis," 88.

8. Morton, *Moving Up without Losing Your Way*, 110.

9. Morton, *Moving Up without Losing Your Way*, 19 (italics in original).

10. Morton, *Moving Up without Losing Your Way*, 84.

11. Morton, *Moving Up without Losing Your Way*, 90.

12. Morton, *Moving Up without Losing Your Way*, 128.

13. Morton, *Moving Up without Losing Your Way*, 128.

14. Archer, "Morphogenesis," 88–89.

15. Archer, "Morphogenesis," 92.

16. Stanley Fish, "Save the World on Your Own Time," *The Chronicle of Higher Education*, 23 January 2003, C5.

17. John Templeton Foundation, ed., *Colleges that Encourage Character Development* (Radnor, PA: Templeton Foundation Press, 1999).

18. Two pluralistic universities that have tried to set forth a robust approach to character education in a pluralistic context are Oxford University (at the graduate level) and Wake Forest University (at the undergraduate level). See Jonathan Brant, Michael Lamb, Emily Burdett, and Edward Brooks, "Cultivating Virtue in Postgraduates: An Empirical Study of the Oxford Global Leadership Initiative," *Journal of Moral Education* 49, no. 4 (2020): 415–35.

19. See Warren Nord, *Does God Make a Difference? Taking Religion Seriously in Our Schools and Universities* (New York: Oxford, 2011) and Perry L. Glanzer and Todd C. Ream, *Christianity and Moral Identity in Higher Education: Becoming Fully Human* (New York: Palgrave Macmillan, 2009).

20. Perry L. Glanzer, Jonathan P. Hill, and Byron R. Johnson, *The Quest for Purpose: The Collegiate Search for a Meaningful Life* (Albany: State University of New York Press, 2017).

21. For a review of this literature see Glanzer et al., *The Quest for Purpose*.

22. Glanzer et al., *The Quest for Purpose*.

23. Morton, *Moving Up without Losing Your Way*; Alasdair MacIntyre, *After Virtue*, 3rd ed. (South Bend, IN: University of Notre Dame Press, 2007).

24. Perry L. Glanzer, *The Quest for Russia's Soul: Evangelicals and Moral Education in Post-Communist Russia* (Waco, TX: Baylor University Press, 2002).

25. Paulo Freire, *Pedagogy of the Oppressed*, trans. Myra Bergman Ramos (New York: Bloomsbury, 2015).

26. The Universal Declaration of Human Rights (1948), article 26 (3), retrieved August 9, 2020 from http://www.un.org/en/documents/udhr/index.html.

Conclusion

The Humanizing Imago Dei University

Identity is not something we inherit.

—Kate C. McLean[1]

Be fully aware, O beautiful soul, of the fact that you are the image of God.

—Saint Ambrose[2]

An important reality for nearly every faith-based university in North America—Catholic, Eastern Orthodox, Jewish, Mormon, and Protestant—is that humans do not define everything about themselves. Contra Kate McLean's claim that "identity is a construction" and "not something we inherit," God our creator, defines our fundamental identity and provides an identity inheritance.[3] On the human quest to discover and develop identity, the discovery that God fundamentally defines who we are can bring tremendous relief and insight.

Indeed, when interviewing a Christian student about the role of Christianity in shaping their ordering of identities, they note, "It's given me a very clear, 'This is what I'm meant to do,' and that's sort of the outline, and then I color in between the lines. I think someone who didn't have that, it would be a lot more confusing and intimidating to try to come up with the whole image and the colors in between." Their use of the term "image" is actually quite consistent with Judeo-Christian thought.

Christians believe there is a blueprint, a basic architectural design that helps people make sense of themselves. It is, in fact, an image. As Genesis 1:27, states, "Then God said, 'Let us make humankind in our image, according to our likeness. . . . ' So God created humankind in his image, in the image

149

of God he created them; male and female he created them" (NRSV). People receive their foremost identity, being made in God's image, from God.[4]

If this divine image is truly one's identity, it has enormous implications for education regarding identity excellence. Christian professors understand this point. A survey of more than 2,300 professors at forty-six different Christian universities in the United States asked them to provide examples of how they integrated the Christian intellectual tradition with their teaching.[5] One of the most dominant ways professors understood Christianity's influence on their teaching can be summarized in one professor's words: "Students and professors alike are image bearers." Another professor wrote, "Students are viewed as whole persons, image bearers of God." What does it then mean to be created in the image or likeness of God?

THE ENRICHING IMPLICATIONS OF
BEING MADE IN GOD'S IMAGE

Christian and Jewish thinkers have discussed this matter for thousands of years and agree on one obvious implication. Both maintain that if made in God's image, one cannot *fully* understand what it means to be a whole person without knowing God, God's story, and humans' relationship to God.[6] For example, John Kilner proposes that being made in God's image—at the highest level—means two things:

> Being made in God's image is about humanity's special connection with God, which God *intends* to result in people's reflection of God in many ways. Those intended likenesses include reason, righteousness, rulership, relationship, and many other human attributes that are praiseworthy. . . . Humanity in God's image is about connection and reflection—a special connection with God intended to reflect attributes of God, to God's glory and for the flourishing of people as God as always intended them to be.[7]

Kilner pinpoints two important, but notably distinct implications: a special connection and a reflection of the divine.

A Special Connection and Relationship

First, being made in God's image, according to the biblical contexts, means humans share a special connection and relationship with God. It is important to recognize that, biblically, all people—no matter their sinfulness or whether they have cultivated certain human capacities or excellences such as reasoning ability—are granted this status by nature of their humanity.[8] As Genesis

9:6 indicates, the fall did not take away the fact that humans are made in God's image. Rather, the imago Dei is given by God's common grace.

What does this claim mean for identity excellence? As chapter 3 revealed, it has meant that all people, whether poor, handicapped, different gender, etc. have equal dignity. As one of the Christian professors surveyed stated, "Every person is made in God's image. . . . We are all valuable and have gifts from Him."[9] Indeed, surveyed educators focused especially on the matter of worth and dignity. One teacher shared, "I strive to treat my students as individuals created in God's image and therefore with intrinsic worth." Still another noted, "All students are created in the image of God and deserve to be treated with respect."

The idea that all humans are made in God's image gives both teachers and students alike a source of worth not related to performance or status in other identities. Human dignity must have a source more fundamental—and external—than human social interpretation. Otherwise, dignity itself becomes susceptible to abuse, being defined and redefined by a shifting society. Thus, to be universal, dignity must come from one's status as image bearers of God.

Acquiring God's Virtue

Kilner's second important stated implication builds on the dignity that comes from a special connection, and yet is distinct from it. God *intends* for us to reflect his nature in many ways. Another biblically faithful interpretation of the imago Dei suggests that all human beings are meant to be physical representations of God here on earth.[10] This part of the image defines human potential. Like a seed, we do not see the full image of the large tree which the seed is capable of producing. Reflecting God's image involves developing and exercising the various aspects of our capacities that reflect God's already existing capacities.[11] In doing so, an individual can grow into a beautiful tree filled with fruit.

Part of this potential is that all humans should develop God's virtue and character to flourish. If humans are made in God's image, then some of their highest order capacities involve moral awareness and judgment, the formation of virtues, and interpersonal communion and love.[12] The language of virtue is one of the primary forms of language used to depict God, who is described as "compassionate, gracious, slow to anger, abounding in love and faithfulness, forgiving, just, holy" (Exodus 34:6–7).[13]

In other words, just as God is holy, people are to be holy. A central New Testament motif is that Christians should imitate Christ—particularly his self-sacrificial love—but also his forgiveness, servant leadership, humility, and acceptance.[14] If universities in the Jewish and Christian traditions seek to develop students to their highest capacities, they must help students cultivate particular virtues, especially agape love that is properly ordered to God.

Recently, Bill Gates, the founder of Microsoft, hosted a video contest asking entrants to answer the question, "What does it mean to be human?" The winner selected by a group of teachers and students was an eighteen-year-old freshman who explained that what makes humans more evolved than ducks and elephants is that they can extend compassion beyond their own immediate circle to "all of humankind," thus sharing "an infinite circle of compassion" and demonstrating "a responsibility to ourselves, to our planet, and to each other."[15]

It is no wonder this student won. As Jonathan Edwards maintained in *The Nature of True Virtue*, extending love to all of creation is what God does. It is also the pinnacle of what makes a person human. Christian Smith places interpersonal love at the top of his list of capacities related to what it means to be human. Such a prioritization reflects the Apostle Paul's claim that the greatest virtue is love, it is "the most excellent way" (I Cor. 12: 21b;13:13b).

Secondary Social Identities

In Genesis 1, God also imbues humanity with unique identities (e.g., male and female) and gives each the capacity to take upon themselves other created identities. In other words, one of the other aspects of being human involves the social identities, both those inherited and those created or chosen. Similarly, scripture continually reveals God to humankind through these social roles and images. God's character is revealed through the roles of particular professions (e.g., potter, shepherd, teacher, etc.). Similarly, God is presented as a king, parent, friend, father, and husband. Of course, these images do not, on their own or collectively, adequately capture the whole of God—just as humans cannot be reduced to a single role or constellation of roles.

Still, with humans, identity is intertwined with social roles. Individuals inherit roles such as that of being a son or daughter, a male or female, and a member of a particular family, race, and nation. Further, individuals take upon themselves other identities, such as being a spouse, parent, a member of a certain profession, a member of various social groups, and more. While these identities do not define a person completely, they do comprise an essential part of each person. A component of the divine calling is to fulfill those roles creatively, to steward them as best as able, and to pursue truth, goodness, and beauty within them.

RELATED TO JESUS CHRIST—THE
IMAGE OF THE INVISIBLE GOD

For the Christian, the grand quest to discover oneself—to understand what it means to be a whole person—begins and ends with God. Ultimately, knowing oneself requires knowing God, and knowing God's love is paramount to knowing what true love is. Christians believe, as Colossians states, "Christ is the image of the invisible God" (Col. 1:15). Consequently, to know a visible image of the invisible God requires knowing Christ. Again, Comenius is helpful. He writes in his famous theology of education, *The Great Didactic*, "Christ, the son of the living God, has been sent from heaven to regenerate in us the image of God . . . now he has been called . . . the archetype of all who are to be formed in the image of God."[16] Or as C. K. Chesterton said, Christ is "more human than humanity."[17] He is the model.

Redeeming and Modeling Identity

The good news is that Jesus offers to share one aspect of this identity with humanity. As Ephesians 1 states, "In love he predestined us for adoption to sonship through Jesus Christ, in accordance with his pleasure and will." Who are we? By God's grace, we are no longer alienated from God. Through Christ we are now holy and blameless and part of God's family. We are adopted. As one Christian professor said, "I see my students as created in the image of God and loved extravagantly by Him. I love them as brothers and sisters in Christ."

This discovery forms the basis of countless wonderful myths and stories. You are not a pauper, but the son or daughter of a king. An excellent example of this understanding of identity can be found in a recent movie version based on the French author Victor Hugo's *Les Misérables* (1998). In the story, Fantine, a single mother, turns to a life of prostitution to support her daughter, Cossette, who is staying with an innkeeper and his wife. Due to a run-in with an unmerciful law enforcer, she is threatened with imprisonment.

Fortunately, Jean Valjean, a reformed criminal who is now mayor of the town, comes to her rescue by extending her grace and forgiveness. Later that evening, he nurses her in his home. He also tells her that he will seek to bring her daughter to her. Fantine responds by repeating her own fallen identity as well as her daughter's, "But I'm a whore and Cosette has no father." Jean Valjean responds by renarrating her life within the context of the redemptive portion of the Christian story that Christ accomplished for us. He tells Fantine, "She has the Lord. He is her Father. And you are His creation. In His eyes you have never been anything but an innocent and beautiful woman."

Or, as Colossians 1:21–22 tells the story, "Once you were alienated from God and were enemies in your minds because of your evil behavior. But now he has reconciled you by Christ's physical body through death to present you holy in his sight, without blemish and free from accusation." In this regard, Christians are born again, new creations with a new identity. Just as Christ changes Simon's identity to Peter and Saul is transformed into Paul, Christians are given a new identity in Christ. We are no longer alienated from God, but we are now aliens—sojourners and strangers—in the fallen world.

If professors fail to help students discover who they really are as persons, image bearers of God, and potential members of God's family through Christ, they will have neglected to tell students the truth about who they and others really are. They will have neglected to reveal to them the secrets to identity excellence and the important virtues that are necessary for it.

The wisdom and virtues of the mature Christian are not the wisdom and virtues of the world. For example, as MacIntyre notes, humility for Aristotle was a vice. In contrast, Jesus comes as a humble servant to die for the sins of humanity and to reconcile the world to God. Or, as Jesus said in Matthew:

> You know that the rulers of the Gentiles lord it over them, and their high officials exercise authority over them. Not so with you. Instead, whoever wants to become great among you must be your servant, and whoever wants to be first must be your slave—just as the Son of Man did not come to be served, but to serve, and to give his life as a ransom for many. (Matthew 20:25–28)

This relationship between identity and ethics is maintained throughout the New Testament.

There is a fascinating pattern in the New Testament epistles. In most epistles, the first part contains no ethical instruction; it simply sets forth how to understand one's self in light of God's story and what Christ has done for us (see for example, Romans, Ephesians, and Colossians). Only after establishing who we are, the epistle authors proceeded to tell us what we should do in the second part of each.

The Christian university hoping to set forth a vision of identity excellence must take students on this journey of discovery—a journey of discovering who God and Christ are—so that students can know themselves and their purpose on Earth. Only after laying this foundation of identity and purpose can the university equip students with more than competencies for acquiring earthly happiness. In doing so, educators might instill in students the full range of virtues given to image bearers of God so that they, too, may join with Christ in reversing the fall.

This reversal requires a different kind of virtue (e.g., sacrificial love) than what is typically prioritized in our egocentric society. In American character education today, several states have passed laws in support of teaching a variety of virtues. The top three virtues taught are honesty, respect, and responsibility.[18] Studying the former Soviet Union revealed students were taught the virtues of patriotism, hard work, and loyalty.[19]

These are all noble virtues. Interestingly though, certain virtues are missing from these national lists—the same virtues Christ tells us explicitly to imitate—the virtues of humility, servanthood, forgiveness, gentleness, faith, hope, love for one's enemies, and sacrificial love for all. A Christian university represents the identity of Christ. To be like Christ requires imitating the abundant life that Christ modeled.

Ultimately, the imago Dei university prioritizes teaching students to live a life of sacrificial and suffering love. Teaching students that the greatest life is one laid down in love for God and others is the ultimate pinnacle of what it means to be an imago Dei university with a vision of identity excellence. It may involve suffering, and possibly even death, but the goal of whole person education is this ultimate, eternal aim.

Implications for the University

Students are not simply bundles of capacities, future professionals, or citizens of earthly kingdoms. In fact, they are all these and so much more. However, these things are held together and rightly understood in light of the truth that students are made in God's image, reflected most fully in Christ. This relationship gives all students dignity, and for Christians, it places them in an extended family of brothers and sisters in Christ. Moreover, it provides students an understanding of the most important virtues necessary for whole person development, such as love. This recognition of identity also gives students a way to prioritize, connect, and develop the different aspects of their identity.

Thus, imago Dei universities can and should provide students with all the key components of identity excellence, such as:

1. A metaidentity and metanarrative for humanity (i.e., made in God's image). This foundation allows humans to recognize that we do not receive our dignity, value, and worth from other identities (e.g., being a straight-A student, a student-athlete, a particular ethnicity or gender, etc.). It provides the foundational identity that gives dignity to all humans and thus to all their other creation-based identities.
2. A metapurpose. Research on purpose has revealed that theistic students understand purpose as having two levels—the overall purpose of glorifying, loving, and serving God and their own personal purpose they discover in relationship with God.[20]

3. Rules. Judaism and Christianity provide specific rules for specific identities that others without those identities may not share, even though we consider the rules as promoting human flourishing.

4. Intellectual, moral, civic, and performance virtues for various human excellences as well as a prioritization of virtue with some metavirtues emphasized (e.g., love, faith, hope, humility, forgiveness, joy, peace, gentleness, kindness, self-control, holiness, serving, gratitude, generosity, wisdom, etc.). Thus, a Christian university will perhaps contain a community covenant that includes Christian rationales for virtues—even those that are considered more common (e.g., intellectual honesty).

5. Practices for developing these virtues and for prioritizing/directing one's virtues (e.g., worship, prayer, giving, hospitality, confession, etc.).

6. Mentors for specific forms of identity excellence and overall excellence in life (e.g., professors are expected to be life models as well as professional models and students are encouraged to find older mentors in Christian virtue within Christian communities).

7. Models of specific forms of excellence and overall excellence (e.g., what it means to be an excellent professional, citizen, *and* human being, that is, saints). Models are not mere mentors, but people who provide an example worth emulating in a particular area.

8. Practical wisdom—for specific forms of excellence as well as excellence in life as a whole—that leads to greater moral imagination. For example, professors who are experts at being Christian social workers can provide practical wisdom as well as perhaps expand students' moral imaginations.

9. Moral imagination—students are expected to learn moral expertise in all of their various identities, so that they may develop a moral imagination for how to improve various form of identity excellence. In that way, they can become the next generation that invents similar institutions such as universities, hospitals, hospices, and more.

Overall, imago Dei universities can have more focused conversations about the combining and ordering of identities related to virtue and excellence (e.g., what virtues are necessary to be an excellent Christian doctor, friend, student, woman, American, Latina; steward of one's body, culture, and nature; and more). Although this chapter has only provided a summary of a vision for the teaching of identity excellence, it provides a framework upon which to build an ever fuller vision. Christian educators are not simply supplying random capacities and intellectual tools. Rather, educators have a clear foundation and framework from which to build and develop the image of God in humanity.

A CLOSING EXAMPLE OF IDENTITY EXCELLENCE

A decade and a half ago I visited Ukrainian Catholic University (UCU), a relatively new Christian university in postcommunist Europe. I found it, on many fronts, to be modeling what it means to engage in identity excellence. Of course, it started with viewing students as made in God's image. The president at the time told me that to emphasize respect for humans made in God's image started with providing clean bathrooms and classrooms.[21] As someone who taught at three different universities in Russia, I know that these matters were sometimes neglected in the postcommunist context.

As stewards of their environment and culture, leaders also took great care to maintain their campus grounds. As a result, the mayor of L'viv came to them for advice about how to take care of other public grounds. Identity excellence, rooted in a Christian understanding of the imago Dei, modeled excellence in stewardship to the whole city. Perhaps one could tell the cleaning and grounds staff to "just be professional," but if the surrounding ethos and community lack an overarching narrative that motivates and reinforces respect for human dignity, there remains little motivation or imagination for achieving goods internal to professions.

In a different vein, from the start, UCU's stated aim has been to become a model for the reform of post-Soviet higher education, which was notoriously corrupt. Bribery between professors and students was common. Their plan for reform took aim at this problem. According to UCU's literature, "The first goal of the Ukrainian Catholic University has been to provide students with a normal academic life, free from concerns of bribery and cheating."[22]

They appear to have had some success. As an administrator once related to me, "UCU is known to be a corruption-free zone."[23] Ukraine's former prime minister Viktor Fedorovych Yanukovych even declared it one of only two higher education institutions without significant corruption (the other being an Orthodox seminary).[24] What makes it possible for the academy to be "saved" in this context is much more than a narrow identity commitment to professional academic purposes and virtues. It involves a communal commitment to broader human goods, such as human dignity, that are cultivated in the basic practices of the moral community that makes up UCU.

UCU's efforts to provide an example of a corruption-free university in Ukraine are rooted in a moral identity beyond just a commitment to the academic professional tradition, although the results are quite consistent with our Western notion of it. Even the professors outside of the dominant moral tradition recognize this point. Olena Dzhedzhora, a humanities professor at UCU, shared with me how when the university began, they had trouble finding Christian humanities professors since Christians were not allowed to obtain advanced degrees in the former Soviet Union. As a result, they hired a number of non-Christian professors. These professors were treated with dignity, did not have to deal with bribes, found clean classrooms, and were paid decently. As a result, a number progressed on a faith journey to the church, since "these values were soon seen as Catholic."[25]

The view that all are made in God's image led UCU to teach students how to start ministries to those in prison, the homeless, and the handicapped. UCU even gave institutional support to The Emmaus Center, a Branch of L 'Arche that ministers to the mentally handicapped with various students often volunteering. An understanding of Christ's redemption and sacrificial love led students and graduates to start a military chaplaincy, a student chaplaincy, a prison chaplaincy, and orphanages. Students contributed in incredible ways toward a civil society that had been previously nonexistent in Ukraine. Student creativity and initiative had been unleashed for redemptive purposes.[26] The professors also produced leading scholarship.

The vision and motivation for serving their university, disciplines, communities, and country extended beyond mere professional expectation or even being excellent citizens. They served because they had discovered an answer to the question of what it means to be a whole person–an answer that stemmed from their understanding of the triune God. For Christian academic leaders, this outlook changed the vision they set forth. The vision worth having should include more than helping students be happy, good professionals, or good citizens. It sought to help students be enriched and flourishing human beings.

NOTES

1. Kate C. McLean, *The Co-authored Self: Family Stories and the Construction of Personal Identity* (New York: Oxford University Press, 2016), 3.

2. Saint Ambrose, *Hexameron, Paradise, and Cain and Abel*, trans. John J. Savage (Washington, DC: Catholic University Press, 1961), 263.

3. McLean, *The Co-authored Self*.

4. Of course, this claim is debated. An article in *Nature* claimed a few years ago, "With all deference to the sensibilities of religious people, the idea that man was created in the image of God can surely be put aside." Astonishingly, the authors of the *Nature* editorial merely asserted this argument without refuting the existence of God or discussing how humans have no relation to God. It was an extraordinary example of academic hubris that scientists like to take at times. "Evolution and the Brain," *Nature* 447 (June 14, 2007): 753.

5. Perry L. Glanzer and Nathan Alleman, "How Christianity Motivates Christian Educators: And Shapes Their Attitudes towards a Class," in *Handbook of Christianity and Education*, William Jeynes, ed. (Hoboken, NJ: Wiley-Blackwell, 2018), 141–64.

6. Genesis 1:27–28; Genesis 9:6; Romans 8:29; 2 Cor. 4:4; Col. 1:15.

7. John Frederic Kilner, *Dignity and Destiny: Humanity in the Image of God* (Grand Rapids, MI: Eerdmans, 2015), 227.

8. Christian Smith makes the distinction between the ontological reality of persons and the existential realization of capacities. The lack of the latter does not negate the dignity that is owed to the former. Christian Smith, *What Is a Person? Rethinking Humanity, Social Life, and the Moral Good from the Ground Up* (Chicago: University of Chicago Press, 2010).

9. Perry L. Glanzer and Nathan F. Alleman, *The Outrageous Idea of the Christian Teacher* (New York: Oxford University Press, 2019).

10. J. Richard Middleton, *The Liberating Image: The Imago Dei in Genesis 1* (Grand Rapids, MI: Brazos Press, 2005).

11. As Stanley Grenz observes, what it means to be understood in the image of God has been interpreted in three broad ways throughout Christian history: 1. structurally, 2. relationally, and as 3. goal or telos. Historically the structural understanding of the imago Dei as reflecting certain God-like qualities or capacities has focused on two in particular—reason and will. As will be seen from my discussion, I found this focus too narrow. In the relational view, "image" is more of a verb than a noun. Humans have the ability to image God whenever they follow God's will. As will be seen from my discussion, I think this approach can easily be combined with the structural view. In other words, it is only when humans properly image God using the capacities I identify that they bear God's image. The third view sees the image as the goal to which humans are ultimately directed in the future. Again, I think this view can be combined with the other two. In other words, humans, using the capacities I described, can image God at times, but they will never fully image God until the future eschaton. Stanley Grenz, *The Social God and the Relational Self: A Trinitarian Theology of the Imago Dei* (Louisville, KY: Westminster/John Knox Press, 2001), 141–82.

12. Smith, *What Is a Person?*, 54.

13. The ability to demonstrate virtue that is God-imitating should not be reduced to the idea of moral agency (e.g., see Malcolm Jeeves, "The Emergence of Human Distinctiveness: The Story from Neuropsychology and Evolutionary Psychology" in *Rethinking Human Nature: A Multidisciplinary Approach*, ed. Malcolm Jeeves [Grand Rapids, MI: Eerdmans, 2011], 196–98). While moral agency is certainly a part of this ability, what is discussed in this section is the ability to use one's will to demonstrate to some degree a particular virtue in the way God would demonstrate it.

14. For more about this emphasis, see John Howard Yoder, *The Politics of Jesus* (Grand Rapids, MI: Eerdmans, 1972).

15. Gatesnotes, *Gates Notes: The Blog of Bill Gates* (blog), https://www.gatesnotes.com/Big-History.

16. Jon Amos Comenius, *The Great Didactic*, trans. M. W. Keatinge (London: Adam and Charles Black, 1907), 30.

17. C. K. Chesterton, *The Everlasting Man* (Redford, VA: Wilder, 2008), 116.

18. Perry L. Glanzer and Andrew J. Milson, "Legislating the Good: A Survey and Evaluation of Contemporary Character Education Legislation," *Educational Policy* 20, no. 3 (2006): 525–50.

19. Perry L. Glanzer, *The Quest for Russia's Soul: Evangelicals and Moral Education in Post-Communist Russia* (Waco, TX: Baylor University Press, 2002).

20. Perry L. Glanzer, Jonathan P. Hill, and Byron R. Johnson, *The Quest for Purpose: The Collegiate Search for a Meaningful Life* (Albany: State University of New York Press, 2017).

21. Conversation with President Borys Guziak, June 5, 2008.

22. Ukrainian Catholic University, n.d. Unpublished manuscript. Cited in Perry L. Glanzer, "The First Ukrainian Christian University: The Rewards and Challenges of Being an Eastern Anomaly," *Christian Higher Education* 11, 5 (2012): 320–30

23. Personal interview with Ukrainian Catholic University administrator by Perry L. Glanzer, Ukrainian Catholic University, L'viv, Ukraine, June 5, 2008.

24. Personal interview with Ukrainian Catholic University administrator by Perry L. Glanzer, Ukrainian Catholic University, L'viv, Ukraine, June 5, 2008.

25. Olena Dzhedzhora, comments at Conference on Catholic Higher Education in Eastern Europe in L'viv, Ukraine, June 5, 2008.

26. Glanzer, "The First Ukrainian Christian University."

Selected Bibliography

Astin, Alexander W., Helen S. Astin, and Jennifer A. Lindholm. *Cultivating the Spirit: How College Can Enhance Students' Inner Lives.* San Francisco: Jossey-Bass, 2011.

Baxter Magolda, Marcia B. *Making Their Own Way: Narratives for Transforming Higher Education to Promote Self-Development.* Sterling, VA: Stylus Press, 2001.

Blasi, Augusto. *Morality, Moral Behavior, and Moral Development.* Edited by William M. Kurtines and Jacob L. Gewirtz. New York: Wiley, 1984.

Bok, Derek. *Beyond the Ivory Tower: Social Responsibilities of the Modern University* Cambridge, MA: Harvard University Press, 1982.

———. *Our Underachieving Colleges: A Candid Look at How Much Students Learn and Why They Should Be Learning More.* Princeton, NJ: Princeton University Press, 2006.

Boyer, Ernest L., and Arthur Levine. *A Quest for Common Learning.* Washington, DC: The Carnegie Foundation for the Advancement of Teaching, 1981.

Brennan, Jason, and Phillip Magness. *Cracks in the Ivory Tower: The Moral Mess of Higher Education.* New York: Oxford University Press, 2019.

Colby, Anne, Thomas Ehrlich, Elizabeth Beaumont, and Jason Stephens. *Educating Citizens: Preparing America's Undergraduates for Lives of Moral and Civic Responsibility.* San Francisco: Jossey-Bass, 2003.

Colby, Anne, and William Damon. *The Moral Self.* Edited by Gil G. Noam and Thomas E. Wren. Boston: MIT Press, 1993.

Davis, David Brion. *Image of God: Religion, Moral Values and Our Heritage of Slavery.* New Haven, CT: Yale University Press, 2001.

Davis, Michael. *Ethics and the University.* New York: Routledge, 1999.

Ericsson, Anders, and Robert Pool. *Peak: Secrets from the New Science of Expertise.* New York: Houghton Mifflin Harcourt, 2016.

Fish, Stanley. *Save the World on Your Own Time.* New York: Oxford University Press, 2008.

Gibbs, John C. *Moral Development and Reality: Beyond the Theories of Kohlberg, Hoffman, and Haidt,* 4th edition. New York: Oxford University Press, 2019.

Glanzer, Perry L. *The Dismantling of Moral Education: How Higher Education Reduced the Human Identity.* Lanham, MD: Rowman & Littlefield, 2022.

Glanzer, Perry L., and Nathan F. Alleman. *The Outrageous Idea of the Christian Teacher.* New York: Oxford University Press, 2019.

Glanzer, Perry L., and Todd C. Ream. *Christianity and Moral Identity in Higher Education.* New York: Palgrave Macmillan, 2009.

Hunter, James Davison, and Paul Nedelisky. *Science and the Good: The Tragic Quest for the Foundations of Morality.* New Haven, CT: Yale University Press, 2019.

Kilner, John Frederic. *Dignity and Destiny: Humanity in the Image of God.* Grand Rapids, MI: Eerdmans, 2015.

Kohlberg, Lawrence. *The Philosophy of Moral Development: Moral Stages and the Idea of Justice, Essays on Moral Development.* San Francisco: Harper and Row Publishers, 1981.

Lapsley, Daniel. *Moral Psychology.* Boulder, CO: Westview, 1996.

MacIntyre, Alasdair C. *After Virtue a Study in Moral Theory*, 3rd edition. South Bend, IN: University of Notre Dame Press, 2007.

Mayhew, Matthew J., Alyssa N. Rockenbach, Nicholas A. Bowman, Tricia A. D. Seifert, and Gregory C. Wolniak. *How College Affects Students: 21st Century Evidence That Higher Education Works*, volume 3. Hoboken, NJ: John Wiley & Sons, 2016.

McLean, Kate C. *The Co-authored Self: Family Stories and the Construction of Personal Identity.* New York: Oxford University Press, 2016.

Morton, Jennifer M. *Moving Up without Losing Your Way: The Ethical Costs of Upward Mobility.* Princeton, NJ: Princeton University Press, 2019.

Nord, Warren A. *Does God Make a Difference? Taking Religion Seriously in Our Schools and Universities.* Oxford: Oxford University Press, 2010.

Parks, Sharon Daloz. *Big Questions, Worthy Dreams: Mentoring Emerging Adults in Their Search for Meaning, Purpose, and Faith*, revised edition. San Francisco: Jossey-Bass, 2011.

Perry, Jr., William G. *Forms of Intellectual and Ethical Development in the College Years: A Scheme.* San Francisco: Jossey-Bass, 1999/1968.

Reuben, Julie. *The Making of the Modern University: Intellectual Transformation and the Marginalization of Morality.* Chicago: University of Chicago Press, 1996.

Sloan, Douglas. "The Teaching of Ethics in the American Undergraduate Curriculum, 1876–1976." In *Ethics Teaching in Higher Education*, edited by Daniel Callahan and Sissela Bok. New York: Plenum Press, 1980.

Smith, Christian, Kari Christoffersen, Hilary Davidson, and Patricia Snell Herzog. *Lost in Transition: The Dark Side of Emerging Adulthood.* New York: Oxford University Press, 2011.

Smith, Christian. *What is a Person?* Chicago: University of Chicago Press, 2010.

Taylor, Charles. *The Sources of the Self: The Making of Modern Identity*. Cambridge, MA: Harvard University Press, 1989.

Index

About the Author

Perry L. Glanzer (PhD, University of Southern California) is professor of educational foundations at Baylor University and a resident scholar with the Baylor Institute for Studies of Religion. He has coauthored, authored, or edited fourteen books including: *The Dismantling of Moral Education: How Higher Education Reduced the Human Identity*; *Christ Enlivened Student Affairs*; *The Outrageous Idea of Christian Teaching*; *The Quest for Purpose: The Collegiate Search for a Meaningful Life*; *Restoring the Soul of the University: Unifying Christian Higher Education in a Fragmented Age*; *Christian Higher Education: A Global Reconnaissance*; *The Idea of a Christian College: A Reexamination for Today's University*; and *Christianity and Moral Identity in Higher Education: Becoming Fully Human*. In addition, he has written or cowritten more than one hundred journal articles and book chapters on topics related to moral education, faith-based higher education, and the relationship between religion and education. He is currently editor-in-chief of *Christian Scholar's Review* and edits the *Christ Animating Learning* blog. His primary scholarly and teaching interests pertain to moral education and the relationship between Christianity and education.